绿色办奥　共享办奥

开放办奥　廉洁办奥

北京冬奥会会徽

会徽以汉字“冬”为灵感来源，运用中国书法的艺术形态，将厚重的东方文化底蕴与国际化的现代风格融为一体，呈现出新时代的中国新形象、新梦想，传递出新时代中国为办好北京冬奥会，圆冬奥之梦、体育强国之梦，实现“带动三亿人参与冰雪运动”目标，推动世界冰雪运动发展，为国际奥林匹克运动做出新贡献的不懈努力和美好追求。

会徽图形上半部分展现滑冰运动员的造型，下半部分表现滑雪运动员的英姿。中间舞动的线条流畅且充满韵律，代表举办地的山峦、赛场、冰雪滑道和节日飘舞的丝带，为会徽增添了节日喜庆的视觉感受，也象征着北京冬奥会将在中国春节期间举行。

会徽以蓝色为主色调，寓意梦想与未来，以及冰雪的明亮纯洁。红黄两色源自中国国旗，代表运动的激情、青春与活力。

北京冬残奥会会徽

会徽设计秉承展现举办地文化、体现以运动员为中心的理念，将中国书法艺术与冬残奥会体育运动特征结合起来。设计展现了汉字“飞”的动感和力度，巧妙地将其幻化成一个向前滑行、冲向胜利的运动员，同时形象化地展现了轮椅等冬残奥会特殊运动器械形态。

会徽图形上半部分线条刚劲曲折，下半部分柔美圆润，寓意运动员经过顽强拼搏、历经坎坷最终达到目标获得圆满成功。会徽展现了运动员不断飞跃、超越自我、奋力拼搏、激励世界的冬残奥精神。

会徽图形整体充满了昂扬向上的激情，奋进飞跃的动感，色彩丰富，构图完美，象征并激发运动员以坚强的意志作为精神的翅膀，在冬残奥赛场上放飞青春梦想！

Olympic and Paralympic Winter Games Beijing 2022

English Reader

北京冬奥会和冬残奥会

英语知识读本

北京 2022 年冬奥会和冬残奥会组织委员会　编

北京体育大学出版社

策划编辑：王英峰
责任编辑：孙　静
责任校对：韩培付
版式设计：谭德毅

图书在版编目（CIP）数据

北京冬奥会和冬残奥会英语知识读本 / 北京2022年冬奥会和冬残奥会组织委员会编. -- 北京 : 北京体育大学出版社, 2022.1
ISBN 978-7-5644-3605-6

Ⅰ. ①北… Ⅱ. ①北… Ⅲ. ①冬季奥运会－英语－口语－自学参考资料②世界残疾人运动会－英语－口语－自学参考资料 Ⅳ. ①G811.212②G811.228

中国版本图书馆CIP数据核字（2022）第011396号

北京冬奥会和冬残奥会英语知识读本
BEIJING DONGAOHUI HE DONGCANAOHUI YINGYU ZHISHI DUBEN
北京 2022 年冬奥会和冬残奥会组织委员会　编

出版发行：北京体育大学出版社
地　　址：北京市海淀区农大南路1号院2号楼2层办公B-212
邮　　编：100084
网　　址：http://cbs.bsu.edu.cn
发 行 部：010-62989320
邮 购 部：北京体育大学出版社读者服务部 010-62989432
印　　刷：北京瑞禾彩色印刷有限公司
开　　本：710mm × 1000mm　1/16
成品尺寸：170mm × 240mm
印　　张：11.25
字　　数：218 千字
版　　次：2022年1月第1版
印　　次：2022年1月第1次印刷
定　　价：60.00元

北京 2022 年冬奥会和冬残奥会
系列教材编委会

《北京冬奥会和冬残奥会英语知识读本》编审人员

主　　编： 闫　成

主　　审： 张　谦

副 主 编： 万学军　潘志伟　赵伯群　王　风　杨振芳　邢尚杰

执行主编： 闫　翔　郭晓勇

执行副主编： 王英峰　丁　翔　田　慧

撰　　稿： 韩亚辉　胡　旭　王卓君　欧欣蓉　何依蔓　亓顺红　安亚男　张馨心　何海交　宋　阳　杨中团　沈静波　丁　宏

审　　稿： 梅建军　何　飞　何　伟　何　川　查泽妹　彭　萍　段星宇　蒋宝春　孙　肖　丁　宏　张　笛　张　奕　孙一冰　尹莳涵　王悦欣　魏昕烨　贾　姗　李文瑨　薛　城　姚昕雨　陈　嘉　宋俊成

编辑制作： 北京体育大学出版社

校　　对： 北京冬奥组委信息与知识管理（IKM）团队

目 录
Contents

MODULE 1 OLYMPIC MOVEMENT, OLYMPIC & PARALYMPIC WINTER GAMES
单元 1 奥林匹克运动、冬奥会和冬残奥会

MODULE 2 DISCIPLINES OF OLYMPIC WINTER GAMES
单元 2 冬奥会项目

MODULE 1

OLYMPIC MOVEMENT, OLYMPIC &
PARALYMPIC WINTER GAMES

单元 1

奥林匹克运动、冬奥会和冬残奥会

Lesson 1 Evolution of Olympic Games
第一课　奥运会发展足迹

The Olympic Games started thousands of years ago in Greece. No one knows exactly when the first games were held, but they were very different from the modern Olympic Games that we might watch on television. The Greek people thought that physical fitness was very important. The games were a way to celebrate[1] discipline[2] and strength, which they thought was important.

奥运会起源于希腊，已有数千年历史。第一届奥运会举办的确切时间不得而知，但其形式肯定与我们在电视上观看的现代奥运会截然不同。希腊人认为强健的体魄至关重要，同时奥运会所颂扬的纪律性与意志力，也是其推崇的两种品格。

The athletes who competed in the ancient Olympic Games were all men, and only one event <u>made up</u> the entire games. The first recorded[3] Olympic Games occurred[4] in 776 B.C., but other tournaments[5] were probably held before then. The Greeks held the Olympic Games in a religious[6] sanctuary[7] in Olympia. They held the games in this place because they wanted to honour Zeus[8], the king of the Greek gods. The single event was a 630-foot race, and an athlete named Coroebus won. This race was the only event for the first 13 games.

古代奥运会的参赛运动员全部是男性，而且只举行一项比赛。虽然有史料记载的第一届奥运会于公元前 776 年举办，但在此之前也可能举办过其他比赛。为了纪念古希腊神话中众神之王宙斯，希腊人选择了在奥林匹亚的宗教圣地举办奥运会，而唯一的项目是 630 英尺赛跑，最终一位名叫科勒布斯的运动员获胜。前 13 届奥运会都是只举办这一项比赛。

New events were eventually[9] <u>added to</u> the Olympic Games. Some of these early events included the hoplitodromos, which actually involved[10] athletes running in a race while wearing a full suit of armour[11]. In 708 B.C., the Greeks added the pentathlon[12], which involved athletes running, jumping, throwing a javelin[13], wrestling, and throwing a discus[14]. In 648 B.C., the pankration[15] was added to the games. This event was a combination[16] of boxing and wrestling that continued until one man

后来，奥运会增加了新的项目。早期项目包括重装步兵赛跑，运动员穿着全套盔甲进行赛跑。公元前 708 年，希腊人将五项全能运动加入奥运会，包括跑步、跳远、投掷标枪、摔跤和投掷铁饼。公元前 648 年，古希腊式搏击进入奥运会。这个项目是拳击和摔跤的结合，

gave up or was knocked unconscious[17]. The Greeks gradually added buildings to the Olympic complex in Olympia. The hippodrome[18] was the arena where runs and chariot[19] races occurred. In the palaestra[20], athletes boxed and wrestled. A separate building was made to house the athletes during the games.

直到一名选手放弃或被打昏时比赛结束。慢慢地，希腊人在奥林匹亚的奥林匹克综合设施内新建了各种建筑。竞技场举行跑步和战车比赛，角力学校举行拳击和摔跤比赛，另外有一栋单独的建筑，供运动员在比赛期间居住。

In 1894, Pierre de Coubertin, a French educator and sportsman, organized a meeting which brought together 79 delegates from 12 countries to discuss how to revive[21] the Olympic Games. The meeting established[22] the first International Olympic Committee (IOC), and the basic idea of having the games every four years was decided upon.

1894 年，法国教育家和运动员皮埃尔·德·顾拜旦组织了来自 12 个国家的 79 名代表开会讨论如何复兴奥运会。那次会议建立了首届国际奥林匹克委员会，并确立了每四年举办一次奥运会的基本思路。

The modern Olympic Games involve both the Summer and Winter Games. Each event is held every four years, but they alternate[23] so that there is an Olympics, either summer or winter, every two years.

现代奥运会包括夏奥会和冬奥会，都是每四年一届，但是会交替举办，即夏奥会和冬奥会交替每隔两年举办一届。

Vocabulary | 词汇

1. celebrate [ˈselɪbreɪt]	*v.*	庆祝；赞美
2. discipline [ˈdɪsəplɪn]	*n.*	纪律，训练
3. record [riˈkɔːd]	*v.*	记录，记载
4. occur [əˈkɜː(r)]	*v.*	发生；出现；存在
5. tournament [ˈtʊənəmənt]	*n.*	锦标赛，联赛
6. religious [rɪˈlɪdʒəs]	*adj.*	宗教的；虔诚的
7. sanctuary [ˈsæŋktʃuəri]	*n.*	圣地；避难所
8. Zeus [zjuːs]	*n.*	宙斯（希腊神话中的主神）
9. eventually [ɪˈventʃuəli]	*adv.*	最后，终于
10. involve [ɪnˈvɒlv]	*v.*	包含；牵涉
11. armour ['aːmə]	*n.*	盔甲；装甲
12. pentathlon [penˈtæθlən]	*n.*	五项全能运动
13. javelin [ˈdʒævlɪn]	*n.*	标枪，投枪
14. discus [ˈdɪskəs]	*n.*	铁饼；掷铁饼
15. pankration [pænˈkreɪʃən]	*n.*	古希腊式搏击
16. combination [ˌkɒmbɪˈneɪʃn]	*n.*	结合；组合
17. unconscious [ʌnˈkɒnʃəs]	*adj.*	无意识的；失去知觉的
18. hippodrome [ˈhɪpədrəʊm]	*n.*	竞技场；跑马场（古希腊）
19. chariot [ˈtʃæriət]	*n.*	二轮战车
20. palaestra [pəˈlestrə]	*n.*	体育场；健身房；角力学校
21. revive [rɪˈvaɪv]	*v.*	使复活，使苏醒
22. establish [ɪˈstæblɪʃ]	*v.*	建立，创立
23. alternate [ɔːlˈtɜːnət]	*v.*	交替；轮流

Language Use | 语言使用

1. make up　　构成，组成；形成

Women officers make up 13 percent of the police force.

女警察构成警力的 13%。

They now make up one in four of the workforce.

目前他们占整个劳动力市场的四分之一。

2. add to　　加入，加到，增加

Do you have anything to add to the list?

你有什么想要添加到列表里吗?

Our explanation seemed only to add to his bewilderment.

我们的解释似乎只是增加了他的困惑。

3. give up　　放弃

She gave up her job to join her husband' s campaign.

她辞了工作以参加丈夫的竞选活动。

In no circumstance should you give up.

无论什么情况，你都不应该放弃。

4. decide upon　　考虑后决定，对……作出决定

How should a graduating student decide upon his future career?

毕业生应该如何决定自己未来的事业?

The most important key to achieving success is to decide upon your goal and get started, take action, move.

获得成功的关键在于：确定目标，立即开始，采取行动，坚定前行。

Lesson 2 Overview of Olympic Winter Games

第二课　冬奥会基本概况

In 1899, the first organized international winter sports competition, the Nordic Games, was staged in Sweden, and only the Scandinavian countries competed. Like the Olympics, it was staged there on every four years but always in Sweden. In 1908, Figure Skating made its way into the Summer Olympics in London, though it was not actually held until October, some three months after the other events ended.

In 1911, the IOC proposed the staging of a separate winter competition for the 1912 Stockholm Games, but Sweden, with the intention of protecting the popularity[1] of the Nordic Games, declined. Germany planned an Olympic Winter Games to precede[2] the 1916 Berlin Summer Games, but World War I brought the cancellation of both. At the 1920 Olympics in Antwerp, Belgium, Ice Hockey joined Figure Skating as an official Olympic event, which paved the road toward having a separate Olympic Games for winter sports.

Two years later, the IOC decided to create the "International Winter Sports Week" as part of the 1924 Summer Olympics. It was held in Chamonix, France, and was so successful that in 1925, the IOC altered[3] its charter[4] to formally create the Olympic Winter Games, retroactively[5] making Chamonix the first.

Since then, in more than 90 years from 1924 to 2018, 11 countries in Europe, America and Asia have successfully hosted 23

1899 年，第一届有组织的国际冬季运动赛事即“北欧运动会”在瑞典举行，但只有斯堪的纳维亚国家参加。自此，它像奥运会一样每四年举办一次，但举办地一直固定在瑞典。1908 年，花样滑冰成为伦敦夏季奥林匹克运动会项目，但比赛于 10 月正式开始，约晚于其他比赛三个月。

1911 年，国际奥委会提议 1912 年斯德哥尔摩奥运会单独举办冬季赛事，但为保持北欧运动会的人气，瑞典拒绝了该提议。德国也曾计划在 1916 年柏林夏季奥运会前举办冬奥会，但第一次世界大战导致两者均被取消。在 1920 年比利时安特卫普举行的奥运会上，冰球继花样滑冰之后，成为正式的奥运会项目，为举办单独的冬奥会奠定基础。

两年后，国际奥委会决定创建“国际冬季运动周”，将其作为 1924 年法国夏慕尼奥运会的一部分。该赛事取得了巨大成功，故国际奥委会于 1925 年更改宪章，正式创建冬奥会，并追溯夏慕尼为第一届冬奥会。

自那之后，在 1924 年到 2018 年的 90 多年间，欧洲、美洲和亚洲的共 11

Olympic Winter Games. Whether it is from the number of countries and regions attending the Olympic Winter Games, or from the number of competition events, or from the number of athletes participating in the Olympic Winter Games, the scale of the Olympic Winter Games has continued to expand.

个国家成功举办了 23 届冬奥会。无论是从参赛国家和地区及竞赛项目的数量，还是从参赛运动员数量来看，冬奥会的规模都在不断扩大。

In the prevailing trend of social development, the Olympic Winter Games will continue to evolve and transform itself as the world' s greatest winter sporting event. In recent years, the pace of adaptive changes in the Olympic Winter Games has accelerated[6]. Nearly half of the 102 events in the 2018 PyeongChang Olympic Winter Games had never been seen in the Nagano Olympic Winter Games 20 years ago or have undergone major adjustments on previous ones.

在社会发展的大趋势下，作为世界上最伟大的冬季运动赛事，冬奥会也将持续发展和变革。近年来，冬奥会的适应性变化步伐加快。在 2018 年平昌冬奥会的 102 个项目中，有将近一半未在 20 年前的长野冬奥会上出现过，或与之前相比进行了重大调整。

Vocabulary | 词汇

1. popularity [pɒpjuˈlærəti] *n.* 人气，普及
2. precede [prɪˈsiːd] *v.* 在……之前发生或出现，先于
3. alter [ˈɔːltə] *v.* 改变，更改
4. charter [ˈtʃɑːtə] *n.* 宪章，纲领
5. retroactively [retrəʊˈæktɪvlɪ] *adv.* 追溯地
6. accelerate [əkˈseləreɪt] *v.* 加速，加快

Language Use | 语言使用

1. with the intention of 抱有……目的，打算

   He went to Paris with the intention of learning French.

   他去巴黎，目的是学法语。

2. pave the road toward 为……铺平道路，为……做好准备

   This agreement will pave the road toward a lasting peace.

   这个协议将为持久和平铺平道路。

Lesson 3 China's Journey through Olympic Winter Games

第三课　中国参与冬奥会的历程

In the 1980 Olympic Winter Games held in Lake Placid, USA, China made its Winter Olympic debut[1], sending 28 athletes to compete in five sports. Wang Guizhen was 18th in the Slalom[2].

在 1980 年美国普莱西德湖冬奥会上，中国首次亮相冬奥会，派出 28 名运动员参加了 5 个分项的角逐。王桂珍获得高山滑雪女子小回转项目第 18 名。

As of the 1984 Olympic Winter Games, China returned to compete in Sarajevo, Yugoslavia, sending 37 athletes to represent the country in the same five disciplines as in 1980.

在 1984 年在南斯拉夫萨拉热窝举办的冬奥会上，中国派出了 37 名运动员，与 1980 年一样，参加了 5 个分项的比赛。

In the 1988 Olympic Winter Games celebrated in Calgary, Canada, Short Track Speed Skating was first introduced as a demonstration[3] sport, and China's Li Yan won the Women's 1000 m and finished third in the 500 m and 1500 m events.

短道速滑在 1988 年加拿大卡尔加里冬奥会上作为表演项目首次亮相，中国选手李琰获得该项目女子 1000 米第一名及 500 米、1500 米第三名。

In the 1992 Olympic Winter Games, China's first-ever Winter Olympic medal went to speed skater Ye Qiaobo, who finished second in the Women's 500 m Final. Chinese short track speed skater Li Yan also won silver in the Women's 500 m Final. Figure skater Chen Lu ranked 6th in the Ladies' Singles at the age of 15. It was the first time for Chinese athletes to rank top six in Figure Skating in the Olympic Winter Games.

在 1992 年法国阿尔贝维尔冬奥会上，中国速度滑冰选手叶乔波夺得速度滑冰女子 500 米银牌，为中国赢得了冬奥历史上的首枚奖牌。李琰获得短道速滑女子 500 米银牌。年仅 15 岁的陈露获得了花样滑冰女子单人赛第 6 名，成为中国在冬奥会上第一个跻身花样滑冰前 6 名的运动员。

In the 1994 Olympic Winter Games held in Lillehammer, Norway, Zhang Yanmei won silver in Women's 500 m Final; Ye Qiaobo won a bronze medal in the Women's 1000 m Speed Skating. Figure skater Chen Lu also won bronze in the Ladies' Singles, making her one of China's youngest-ever medal winners in Figure Skating for China.

在 1994 年挪威利勒哈默尔冬奥会上，张艳梅在短道速滑女子 500 米决赛中收获银牌；叶乔波获得速度滑冰女子 1000 米铜牌；陈露获得花样滑冰铜牌，成为中国花样滑冰在冬奥会历史上最年轻的获得奖牌的选手。

In the 1998 Olympic Winter Games (Nagano, Japan), the honour went to short track speed skater Li Jiajun, who won silver in the Men' s 1000 m. Fellow speed skater An Yulong won silver in the Men' s 500 m. The Short Track Speed Skating event saw Yang Yang (S) win a hat-trick of silver medals in the Women' s 1000 m, 500 m and 3000 m relay.

In the 2002 Olympic Winter Games (Salt Lake City, United States), China won its first-ever Winter Olympic gold medal, quickly followed by its second. Both were won by short track speed skater Yang Yang, first in the Women' s 500 m and then the 1000 m. It wasn' t only Speed Skating events that brought China medals. Figure skaters Shen Xue and Zhao Hongbo won bronze in the pairs event.

In the 2006 Olympic Winter Games (Turin, Italy), the Chinese Short Track and Speed Skating teams were in excellent form. The first gold of 2006–and the first of her career–was won by Wang Meng in the 500m short track. Han Xiaopeng became the first Chinese male athlete to ever win a gold medal at the Olympic Winter Games of the Men' s Freestyle Aerials[4] Final.

The 2010 Olympic Winter Games (Vancouver, Canada) figure skaters Shen Xue and Zhao Hongbo finally won China' s first gold in the pairs, setting a world record for the overall combined score in the process. Wang Meng became the first and only Chinese athlete to ever win three Olympic Winter Games golds at a single Games, which came in the 500 m, 1000 m and 3000 m relay.

The 2014 Olympic Winter Games (Sochi, Russia) short track speed skater Li Jianrou won the Women' s 500 m and claimed[5] the honour of winning China' s 10th Winter Olympic gold medal. Zhou Yang followed

在 1998 年日本长野冬奥会上，李佳军获得短道速滑男子 1000 米银牌；安玉龙在男子 500 米速滑项目上也勇夺银牌。而女子短道速滑运动员杨扬则连夺 1000 米、500 米和 3000 米接力 3 枚银牌。

在 2002 年美国盐湖城冬奥会上，杨扬一鸣惊人，在短道速滑女子 500 米决赛中，为中国获得了第一枚冬奥会金牌；随后又在短道速滑女子 1000 米比赛中再夺金牌。当然中国并不只在速度滑冰项目中有奖牌入账，申雪、赵宏博也在花样滑冰双人滑项目中拼下了 1 枚铜牌。

在 2006 年意大利都灵冬奥会上，中国短道速滑和速度滑冰队表现不俗。王濛获得 1 枚短道速滑女子 500 米金牌，这是 2006 年冬奥会中国代表队的首金，也是她职业生涯中的首枚金牌；韩晓鹏在自由式滑雪男子空中技巧项目决赛中赢得金牌，夺得了中国男选手的首枚冬奥会金牌。

在 2010 年加拿大温哥华冬奥会上，申雪和赵宏博在双人滑项目上第一次夺得冠军，总成绩打破了世界纪录。王濛夺得了 500 米、1000 米和 3000 米接力的金牌，成为首位也是唯一在一届冬奥会上获得 3 枚金牌的中国运动员。

在 2014 年俄罗斯索契冬奥会上，短道速滑选手李坚柔获得女子 500 米项目的金牌，成为中国获得第 10 枚冬奥会金牌的运动员；周洋则紧随其后，在女子

suit, picking up gold in the 1500m final and then Fan Kexin won silver in the 1000m. Zhang Hong managed to beat other speed skaters in the 1000m to claim victory.

In the 2018 Olympic Winter Games (PyeongChang, the ROK), China did, however, win its first-ever Olympic medal in Snowboard after Liu Jiayu picked up silver in the Women' s Halfpipe. They also won two medals in the Freestyle Skiing, with Zhang Xin winning silver. In the Men' s 500m, short track speed skater Wu Dajing won gold in the Men' s 500m final, setting a world-record time of 39.584 seconds.

Including PyeongChang 2018, China has participated in 11 Olympic Winter Games and collected 13 gold, 28 silver and 21 bronze medals, placing it 16th in the overall ranking.

1500 米决赛中获得金牌；范可新获得女子 1000 米银牌。最大惊喜是张虹夺得了速度滑冰女子 1000 米冠军。

在 2018 年韩国平昌冬奥会上，刘佳宇获得单板滑雪女子U型场地决赛亚军，为中国赢得首枚单板滑雪奖牌；同时，中国也在自由式滑雪项目中赢得两块奖牌，包括张鑫斩获的 1 枚银牌。在短道速滑男子 500 米的决赛中，武大靖获得金牌并创造了 39.584 秒的世界纪录。

截至 2018 年平昌冬奥会，中国体育代表团的冬奥之旅已历经 11 届，共获得 13 枚金牌、28 枚银牌、21 枚铜牌，在奖牌榜排名第 16 位。

Vocabulary | 词汇

1. debut [ˈdebjuː]	*n. / v.*	初次登台，开张
2. Slalom [ˈslɑːləm]	*n.*	回转
3. demonstration [ˌdemənˈstreɪʃn]	*n.*	示范
4. Aerial [ˈeəriəl]	*adj.*	空中的
5. claim [kleɪm]	*v.*	要求，声称，认领

Language Use | 语言使用

1. make one' s debut　首次登场，初次登场

   The band made their debut last week.

   乐队上周进行了首秀。

2. claim the honour　获得荣誉

   Yao claimed the honour of the Best Male Athlete.

   姚问鼎最佳男运动员。

Lesson 4 Overview of Paralympic Winter Games

第四课　冬残奥会基本情况

In 1948, Sir Ludwig Guttmann organised a sports competition involving World War II veterans[1] with a spinal cord-related injury in Stoke Mandeville, England. Four years later, competitors from Holland joined the Games, and the international movement, now known as the Paralympic Movement, was born.

1948 年，路德维希·古特曼爵士在英格兰的斯托克·曼德维尔组织了一场由脊柱受伤的“二战”老兵参加的体育赛事。四年后，来自荷兰的运动员也加入了该运动会，于是这项国际运动，也就是现在的残奥运动诞生了。

Olympic-style games for athletes with a disability were organised for the first time in Rome in 1960. In Toronto in 1976, other disability groups were added, and the idea of merging[2] together different disability groups for international sports competitions was born. In the same year, the first Paralympic Winter Games took place in Sweden. <u>Hot on the heels</u> of the Olympic Winter Games come the Paralympic Winter Games. The incredible[3] athletes have each overcome a disability to compete at the highest level. The Paralympic Winter Games are also hosted by the city that hosted the Olympic Winter Games. The International Paralympic Committee (IPC) oversees[4] the Paralympic Winter Games.

1960 年，罗马首次为残疾人运动员举办了奥运会式的运动会。1976 年在多伦多，其他残疾人团体加入该运动会，并且将不同的残疾人团体合并在一起参加国际体育比赛的思想产生。同年，第一届冬残奥会在瑞典举行。冬奥会结束后，紧接着冬残奥会举办。这些了不起的运动员克服了身体残疾的障碍，展现出最高水平的比赛。冬残奥会也由举办冬奥会的城市主办。国际残奥委会（IPC）负责管理冬残奥会。

The sports at the Paralympic Winter Games include Alpine Skiing, Biathlon, Cross-Country Skiing, Para Ice Hockey, Wheelchair Curling and Para Snowboard.

冬残奥会的运动项目包括高山滑雪、冬季两项、越野滑雪、残奥冰球、轮椅冰壶和残奥单板滑雪等。

To ensure competition is fair and equal, all Paralympic sports have a system in place which ensures that winning is determined by skill, fitness, power, endurance, tactical ability and mental focus, the same

为了确保比赛公平公正，所有残奥会项目都有一套确保根据技能、体能、爆发力、耐力、战术能力和精神集中度来定胜负的制度，而这些也是身体正常

factors that account for success in sport for able-bodied athletes.

运动员取得成功的因素。

In each Paralympic sport, the criteria of grouping athletes by the degree of activity limitation resulting from the impairment are named “Sport Classes”. Through classification, it is determined which athletes are eligible to compete in a sport and how athletes are grouped together for competition. This, to a certain extent, is similar to grouping athletes by age, gender or weight.

在每个残奥会项目中，根据残疾导致的活动受限程度对运动员进行分组的标准称为“体育分级”。通过分级，可以确定哪些运动员有资格参加某一项运动，以及如何将运动员分组进行比赛。在某种程度上，这类似于按年龄、性别或体重对运动员进行分组的做法。

Classification is sport-specific because an impairment affects the ability to perform at different degrees in different sports. As a consequence, an athlete may meet the criteria in one sport, but may not in another.

分级按项目展开，因为残疾对不同项目中的表现能力的影响也不同。因此，一名运动员可能符合某一个项目的标准，但却不符合另一个项目的标准。

Vocabulary | 词汇

1. veteran [ˈvetərən] *n.* 退役军人，老兵
2. merge [mɜːdʒ] *v.* 合并
3. incredible [ɪnˈkredəbl] *adj.* 令人难以置信的
4. oversee [ˌəʊvəˈsiː] *v.* 监管

Language Use | 语言使用

hot on the heels 紧跟着，接踵而至

He turned and fled with Peter hot on the heels.

他转身逃跑，彼得紧追不舍。

Lesson 5 China's Journey through Paralympic Winter Games

第五课 中国参与冬残奥会的历程

China first competed at the Paralympic Winter Games in 2002. Han Lixia ranked[1] the sixth in the Women's 10 km Free Technique Cross-Country Skiing in Salt Lake City, US.

In the Women's 3×2.5 km Relay Open Cross-Country Skiing competition at the 2006 Turin Paralympic Winter Games, Han Lixia, Zhang Nannan and Peng Yuanyuan won the 8th place.

China sent 7 competitors to compete in one discipline at the 2010 Paralympic Winter Games in Vancouver, Canada. Peng Yuanyuan ranked the 5th in the 5 km Classic, Standing and 7th in the 15 km Free, Standing Cross-Country Skiing. Zou Dexin, Fu Chunshan and Cheng Shishuai won 8th in the 1×4 km + 2×5 km Relay Cross-Country Skiing.

In the Sochi 2014 Paralympic Winter Games, China's Wheelchair Curling[2] team, led by Wang Haitao, won the 4th place in the competition.

Despite having competed at every Winter Games since Salt Lake City in 2002, China did not win a single medal until at the 2018 Paralympic Winter Games, where China won their first ever gold medal as well as the first medal in the Wheelchair Curling competition. On 17 March 2018, Wang Haitao, Chen Jianxin, Liu Wei, Wang Meng and Zhang Qiang won the first ever Paralympic Winter Games gold medal as well as the first ever Paralympic Winter Games medal for China. Liu Sitong

中国在 2002 年冬残奥会上首次参加比赛。韩丽霞在美国盐湖城的女子 10 公里自由技术越野滑雪中排名第六。

在 2006 年都灵冬季残奥会的女子 3×2.5公里公开级接力越野滑雪比赛中，韩丽霞、张楠楠和彭园园获得了第八名。

中国派出了 7 名选手参加 2010 年加拿大温哥华冬残奥会的一个分项比赛。彭园园在越野滑雪 5 公里传统技术站姿比赛中排名第五，在越野滑雪 15 公里自由技术站姿比赛中排名第七。邹德新、付春山和程世帅在越野滑雪 1×4 公里 +2×5 公里接力赛中获得第八名。

2014 年，由王海涛率领的中国轮椅冰壶队在索契冬残奥会比赛中获得第四名。

虽然中国参加了自 2002 年盐湖城以来的每一届冬残奥会，但一直颗粒无收。直到 2018 年冬残奥会，中国获得了有史以来的第一枚金牌，也是轮椅冰壶项目的第一枚奖牌。2018 年 3 月 17 日，王海涛、陈建新、刘薇、王蒙和张强获得了中国第一枚冬残奥会金牌，这也是中国在冬残奥会历史上的第一枚金牌。刘思彤在高山滑雪女子回转坐姿项目中排

ranked 6th in the Women' s Slalom, Sitting Alpine Skiing[3]; Zheng Peng won the 4th place in the Men' s 15 km Free, Sitting Cross-Country Skiing.

名第六。郑鹏在越野滑雪男子 15 公里自由技术坐姿比赛中获得第四名。

The preparations for the Beijing 2022 Paralympic Winter Games are progressing well on all fronts as the venue construction is on schedule and many legacy venues from Beijing 2008 Games will be used for the Beijing 2022 Games, while all new venues will be built with sustainability in mind. The hosting of the Olympic and Paralympic Winter Games would sure be a valuable opportunity for China to develop its winter sports.

北京 2022 年冬残奥会的筹办工作在各方面进展顺利，场地建设如期进行，北京 2008 年奥运会的很多场馆将用于 2022 年冬奥会和冬残奥会，而所有新建场馆都会考虑可持续性。冬奥会和冬残奥会的举办对于中国发展冬季运动无疑是一个宝贵的机会。

Vocabulary | 词汇

1. rank [ræŋk] *v.* 排名
2. Wheelchair Curling 轮椅冰壶
3. Sitting Alpine Skiing 高山滑雪坐姿

Language Use | 语言使用

on all fronts 各条战线，在各方面

Reports of success on all fronts came in quick succession.

全国各条战线纷纷报喜。

Lesson 6 Bid for the 2022 Olympic Winter Games

第六课　申办 2022 年冬奥会

On 15 January 2014, the Beijing 2022 Olympic Winter Games Bid Committee was launched. With the strong support from Beijing municipal government, Hebei provincial government, and General Administration of Sport of China, the Bid Committee, with passion and commitment, moved step by step towards the Olympic goal.

The Committee worked day and night to complete the *Application File*[1], defining the vision and a general framework for the 2022 Winter Games. Meanwhile, Beijing started to tackle sustainability[2] and environmental challenges, demonstrating its desire and determination to deliver a successful 2022 Games. For example, it has taken concrete actions to tackle air pollution, which was identified as one of the major challenges for the bidding.

On 7 July 2014 the IOC announced the cities selected into Phase II as Candidate Cities[3], with Beijing, Oslo, and Almaty entering the second round.

Such success <u>injected[4] confidence into</u> the Bid Committee. They recruited more than 200 experts and scholars from government departments, universities and research institutions to compile the *Candidature File*[5]. The file, compiled by 205 people altogether, contains 3 volumes and 14 topics, further outlining the blueprint for the Olympic Winter Games Beijing 2022 on the basis of the *Application File*. It embodies the philosophy of *Olympic Agenda 2020* and ensures that the important concept of running an athlete-centred, economical and sustainable

2014 年 1 月 15 日，北京 2022 年冬奥会申办委员会（简称“冬奥申委”）成立。在北京市政府、河北省政府和国家体育总局的大力支持下，冬奥申委带着热情和决心一步步迈向奥林匹克梦想。

冬奥申委夜以继日地撰写《申办城市申请文件》，确定北京 2022 年冬奥会的愿景和总体框架。同时，北京也开始应对可持续发展和环境领域的挑战，表现出了争取成功举办 2022 年冬奥会的愿望和决心。例如，空气污染是北京申办冬奥会所面临主要的挑战之一，因此北京采取了切实有效的措施治理空气污染。

2014 年 7 月 7 日，国际奥委会宣布进入申奥第二阶段的候选城市，北京、奥斯陆和阿拉木图成功入围。

成功入围候选城市让冬奥申委信心倍增。他们从政府部门、高校和科研机构抽调了超过 200 名专家学者撰写《申办报告》。该报告由 205 人共同撰写，包括 3 卷共 14 个主题，在《申办城市申请文件》的基础上进一步描绘了 2022 年冬奥会的蓝图，充分体现了《奥林匹克 2020 议程》的思想，确保在申办和举办

Games will be represented well in Beijing' s bid and actual organisation of the Games in 2022.

冬奥会的过程中都能突出“以运动员为本、可持续发展和节俭办赛”的理念。

In January 2015, Beijing officially submitted the *Candidature File* to the IOC. It was time for the final sprint!

2015 年 1 月，北京正式向国际奥委会提交了《申办报告》。到了最后冲刺的时候了！

The Beijing 2022 Olympic Winter Games Bid Committee made full preparations for the final presentation, assembling an all-star team of presenters to show the world Beijing' s capacity to stage the winter sports gala[6]. It carefully selected the presenters, with eight women accounting for almost half of the team, tailored[7] every speech according to different speakers, brainstormed every possible question that might come up during the question and answer session, and rehearsed[8] repeatedly for further improvement.

冬奥申委为最终陈述做了充足的准备，并集结了一支全明星团队向世界展示北京举办冬季体育盛会的能力。陈述人都经过精心遴选，其中女性达到 8 人，占半数以上；每一份陈述稿都根据陈述人情况量身打造；对问答环节可能出现的问题进行预测并斟酌答题口径，反复演练，不断提高。

On 31 July 2015, Beijing made a spectacular[9] final presentation in the 128th IOC Session. At the end of the session, a total of 85 IOC members cast their ballots. Beijing received 44 votes, while Almaty received 40, a narrow victory indicating[10] just how fierce the competition was.

2015 年 7 月 31 日，北京申奥代表团在国际奥委会第 128 次全会上呈现了一场高水平的陈述。陈述结束之后，共 85 名国际奥委会委员进行了投票。北京获得 44 票，阿拉木图获得 40 票，票数之接近足以看出竞争之激烈。

This was indeed a historic[11] moment. Beijing, a city that staged the Summer Olympic Games, is about to become the first city ever to host both the Summer and the Winter Games in more than a century of Olympic history!

这的确是一个历史性的时刻。举办过夏季奥运会的北京即将成为奥运史上第一个既举办夏奥会又举办冬奥会的双奥城市！

Vocabulary | 词汇

1.	Application File		申办城市申请文件
2.	sustainability [səˌsteɪnəˈbɪləti]	*n.*	可持续性
3.	Candidate City		候选城市
4.	inject [ɪnˈdʒekt]	*v.*	注入
5.	Candidature File		申办报告
6.	gala [ˈgɑːlə]	*n.*	盛会
7.	tailor [ˈteɪlə(r)]	*v.*	专门制作，定制
8.	rehearse [rɪˈhɜːs]	*v.*	彩排，演练
9.	spectacular [spekˈtækjələ(r)]	*adj.*	精彩的，令人印象深刻的
10.	indicate [ˈɪndɪkeɪt]	*v.*	表明，显示
11.	historic [hɪˈstɒrɪk]	*adj.*	有历史意义的，载入史册的

Language Use | 语言使用

1. inject...into...　　把……注入

   The new commercial district injected new life into this area.

   新建的商业区为该地区注入了新的活力。

2. cast a ballot　　投票

   In her late thirties, she cast a ballot for the first time in her life to back Obama, citing healthcare as her biggest concern.

   三十几岁的她投出了人生中第一张票，支持奥巴马，并表示她最关心的是医疗保健。

3. narrow victory　　险胜

   She won a narrow victory over her great rival in the tennis competition.

   她在那次网球赛中险胜了强敌。

Lesson 7 About Olympic and Paralympic Winter Games Beijing 2022

第七课 北京 2022 年 冬奥会和冬残奥会基本情况

In the year of 2022, Beijing, together with its adjacent[1] city of Zhangjiakou, will host the XXIV Olympic Winter Games and the XIII Paralympic Winter Games.

During the Olympic Winter Games Beijing 2022, slated[2] for 4 February through 20 February, a total of 42 venues will be utilised, including 12 competition venues[3], 27 non-competition venues[4] and 3 training venues[5]. Among all these venues, 28 are located in Beijing Zone, 4 in Yanqing Zone, and 10 in Zhangjiakou Zone. During the Paralympic Winter Games, scheduled for 4 March to 13 March, a total of 33 venues will be used.

The Olympic Winter Games Beijing 2022 is to encompass[6] 15 disciplines and 109 events, while the Paralympic Winter Games will feature[7] 6 sports and 78 events.

Up till now, the preparation work has entered the Readiness phase. Venue and infrastructure construction are well underway; competition organisation as well as venue operation are proceeding[8] in order; Games services work such as accommodation, food and beverage, medical service, security and transport is moving forward steadily[9]; Games communication and promotion keeps booming; marketing programme is

2022 年，北京携手其相邻城市张家口将举办第 24 届冬奥会和第 13 届冬残奥会。

北京冬奥会将于 2022 年 2 月 4 日至 20 日举行，计划使用 42 个场馆，包括 12 个竞赛场馆、27 个非竞赛场馆、3 个训练场馆。其中，北京赛区有 28 个场馆、延庆赛区有 4 个场馆、张家口赛区有 10 个场馆。北京 2022 年冬残奥会将于 3 月 4 日至 13 日举办，计划使用 33 个场馆。

北京冬奥会包含 15 个竞赛分项、109 个竞赛小项。北京冬残奥会包含 6 个竞赛大项、78 个竞赛小项。

目前，筹办工作进入到测试就绪阶段。场馆和基础设施建设加快推进，赛事组织和场馆运行工作有序展开，住宿、餐饮、医疗、安保、交通等赛会服务保障扎实推进，宣传与推广工作持续升温，

shaping up nicely; international exchanges and cooperation continue to broaden; and talents development and training has seen great achievements.

市场开发打开良好局面，国际交流合作不断深化，人才开发与培养工作取得丰硕成果。

It is also worth noting that Beijing 2022 has unveiled the emblems of "Winter Dream" and "Flying High" for the Olympic and Paralympic Winter Games, respectively. The mascots of "Bing DwenDwen" for the Olympic Winter Games and "Shuey RhonRhon" for the Paralympic Winter Games are well received by the public.

值得一提的是，北京冬奥组委发布了冬奥会会徽"冬梦"、冬残奥会会徽"飞跃"。冬奥会吉祥物"冰墩墩"、冬残奥会吉祥物"雪容融"，深受大众喜爱。

On 5 December 2019, the 34th International Volunteer Day, Beijing 2022 kicked off its global recruitment of Games volunteers. To date, it has received more than 850,000 applications.

2019 年 12 月 5 日，适逢第 34 个国际志愿者日，北京冬奥组委启动赛会志愿者全球招募工作，目前，已经有超过 85 万人报名申请赛会志愿者。

Vocabulary | 词汇

1. adjacent [əˈdʒeɪsnt]	*adj.*	相邻的，接壤的
2. slate [sleɪt]	*v.*	安排，指定
3. competition venue		竞赛场馆
4. non-competition venue		非竞赛场馆
5. training venue		训练场馆
6. encompass [ɪnˈkʌmpəs]	*v.*	包括，包含
7. feature [ˈfiːtʃə]	*v.*	以……为主要内容
8. proceed [prəˈsiːd]	*v.*	前进，行进
9. steadily ['stedɪlɪ]	*adv.*	持续地，稳固地

Language Use | 语言使用

1. be slated for...　　被预定为……

   Controversial energy measures are slated for Senate debate within days.

   几项颇受争议的能源措施定于几天后提交参议院讨论。

2. up till now...　　截至目前

   Up till now, biological weapons are banned throughout the world.

   到目前为止，国际上一直禁止使用生物武器。

3. be worth noting　　值得注意的是……

   It is worth noting that the inflation rate has been quite low in recent years and relatively stable in comparison with the last 10–20 years.

   值得注意的是，最近几年通货膨胀率保持低位，且较过去 10~20 年相对平稳。

MODULE 2

DISCIPLINES OF OLYMPIC WINTER GAMES

单元 2

冬奥会项目

Lesson 1 Speed Skating
第一课　速度滑冰

Speed Skating is a competitive form of ice skating in which the competitors race each other in travelling a certain distance on skates, while the skater spending the shortest time wins the game. The sport is governed by the International Skating Union (ISU).

速度滑冰是一种滑冰竞技形式，运动员们穿着冰鞋进行一定距离的滑行比赛，用时最短者获胜。国际滑冰联盟（ISU）是速度滑冰运动的管理机构。

The roots of Speed Skating date back over a millennium[1] to Scandinavia, Northern Europe and the Netherlands, where the natives[2] added bones to their shoes and used them to travel on frozen rivers, canals and lakes. The Dutch were arguably the earliest pioneers[3] of skating. They began using canals to maintain communication by skating from village to village as far back as the 13th century. Skating eventually spread across the channel to England, and soon the first clubs and artificial rinks began to form. Passionate[4] skaters included several kings of England, Marie Antoinette, Napoleon III and German writer Johann Wolfgang von Goethe.

速度滑冰可以追根溯源至千年之前的北欧斯堪的纳维亚半岛与荷兰，那里的人们在鞋子上绑上骨头并用它们在冰冻的河流、运河和湖泊上滑行。荷兰人可以说是最早的滑冰先锋。早在 13 世纪，他们就开始利用运河，将滑冰作为村镇间保持联系的交通方式。最终，滑冰运动穿越海峡传到英格兰，很快第一批俱乐部和人造冰场开始形成。英国的几位国王、玛丽·安托瓦内特、拿破仑三世和德国作家约翰·沃尔夫冈·冯·歌德等都非常喜欢滑冰。

The first known skating competition is thought to have been held in the Netherlands in 1676. However, the first official Speed Skating events were not held until 1863 in Oslo, Norway. In 1889, the Netherlands hosted the first World Championships, bringing together Dutch, Russian, American and English teams.

第一场已知的滑冰比赛公认于 1676 年在荷兰举行。然而，第一次正式的速度滑冰比赛直到 1863 年才在挪威奥斯陆举行。1889 年，荷兰举办了第一届速度滑冰世界锦标赛，汇集了来自荷兰、俄罗斯、美国和英国的队伍。

Speed Skating appeared for the first time in 1924 at the first Olympic Winter Games in Chamonix. Initially, only men were allowed to participate. It was only at the Lake Placid Games in 1932 that women were authorised to compete in Speed Skating, which was then only a demonstration sport. It was not until the 1960 Games in Squaw Valley that Women' s event was officially included in the Olympic programme.

The events almost always follow the European system, which consists of skaters competing two-by-two. At the 1932 Olympic Games, the Americans organised American-style events, i.e. with a mass start. This decision brought about a boycott by many European competitors, which allowed the Americans to win the four gold medals.

1924 年，在夏慕尼举办的第一届冬奥会上，速度滑冰就是正式比赛项目，但最初只有男性可以参加。直到 1932 年的普莱西德湖冬奥会，女性才被允许参加速度滑冰比赛，但当时它还只是一个表演项目。最终，在 1960 年斯阔谷冬奥会上，女子速滑项目被正式列入奥运会比赛项目。

速滑比赛几乎一直遵照欧洲体系开展，即运动员两人一组进行比赛。然而在 1932 年的冬奥会上，美国人组织了美式速滑比赛，如多人集体出发的形式。这一决定引起了很多欧洲运动员的抵制，最终美国人赢得了四枚金牌。

Vocabulary | 词汇

1.	millennium [mɪˈleniəm]	*n.*	千年，千年期，千禧年
2.	native [ˈneɪtɪv]	*adj.*	本国的，土著的
3.	pioneer [ˌpaɪəˈnɪə(r)]	*n.*	拓荒者，开发者，先驱者
4.	passionate [ˈpæʃənət]	*adj.*	热烈的，激昂的

Language Use | 语言使用

bring about 造成，引起

We are working to bring about closer political integration in the EU.

我们正在努力实现欧盟内部更加紧密的政治一体化。

Lesson 2 Short Track Speed Skating

第二课　短道速滑

Short Track Speed Skating is an ice discipline. In competitions, multiple skaters (typically between four and six) skate on an oval[1] ice track with a length of 111.12 metres. The ice rink[2] has a minimum measurement of 60 metres × 30 metres.

Short Track Speed Skating was originated from Canada in 1905 when artificial indoor Ice Hockey rinks were built, which led many skaters to practise on ice rinks. In 1979, Quebec City, Winnipeg and other cities in Canada started to hold mass indoor Speed Skating competitions on a short track.

In 1967, the International Skating Union (ISU) adopted Short Track Speed Skating, although it didn' t organise international competitions until 1976. World Championships in Short Track Speed Skating have been officially held since 1981, although

短道速滑是一个冰上运动项目。在比赛中，多名运动员（通常为 4~6 人）在长为 111.12 米的椭圆形冰道上滑行。冰面最小尺寸为 60 米 ×30 米。

短道速滑 1905 年起源于加拿大。当时加拿大修建了室内冰球场，于是一些滑冰爱好者开始在室内冰球场地进行练习。1979 年，加拿大的魁北克市、温尼伯等城市相继组织室内短道速度滑冰比赛。

1967 年，国际滑冰联盟（ISU）接纳了短道速滑项目，但直到 1976 年才开始组织国际比赛。短道速滑世锦赛自 1981 年开始正式举办，不过从 1976 年

events held in 1976–1980 under different names have since received the status of World Championships retrospectively[3]. The name of the competition had been changed several times before it was eventually[4] titled the "World Short Track Speed Skating Championships" in 1989. The championships are now held annually.

到 1980 年，以各种名称举办的短道速滑比赛最终都获得了与世锦赛相同的地位。赛事名称在几经更改后，最终于 1989 年确定为“世界短道速滑锦标赛”。目前该锦标赛每年举行。

Short Track Speed Skating was introduced as a demonstration sport at the 1988 Olympic Winter Games in Calgary in Canada. Short Track Speed Skating officially became part of the Olympic programme in 1992 and has been part of the Olympic Winter Games ever since. There were only four short track events at the 1992 Olympic Winter Games, but the programme was expanded to include six events in 1994 and 1998, and finally eight events at the 2002 Olympic Winter Games. The mixed team relay 2000m will make its debut at the Olympic Winter Games Beijing 2022, while short track discipline will be expanded to nine events.

1988 年，加拿大卡尔加里冬奥会将短道速滑作为表演项目引入。1992 年，短道速滑正式成为奥运项目，此后，它一直是冬奥会比赛项目。在 1992 年冬奥会上，短道速滑只有 4 个小项，到 1994 年和 1998 年时，已增加到 6 个，到 2002 年冬奥会时，最终设立了 8 个小项。北京 2022 年冬奥会新增设混合团体接力项目，将短道速滑项目的小项总数增至 9 项。

Short Track Speed Skating competitions have identical format for men and women: 500 metres, 1000 metres, 1500 metres, plus the relay event (5000 metres for men, 3000 metres for women). A 3000-metre super-final event is included in the European and World Championships, but this is not currently part of the Olympic short track programme.

男女短道速滑的项目包括 500 米、1000 米、1500 米及接力（男子 5000 米，女子 3000 米）比赛。欧洲锦标赛和世界锦标赛还包括超级 3000 米决赛，但其目前尚未纳入冬奥会。

Vocabulary | 词汇

1. oval [ˈəʊvl] *n.* 椭圆形
2. rink [rɪŋk] *n.* 冰场
3. retrospectively [ˌretrəˈspektɪvli] *adv.* 回顾性地
4. eventually [ɪˈventʃuəli] *adv.* 最终

Language Use | 语言使用

be expanded to　　扩大到

That system should be expanded to include all regions.

这个系统应得到扩大从而将所有区域包括在内。

Lesson 3 Figure Skating

第三课　花样滑冰

Figure Skating[1] is a discipline in which ice skaters, singly or <u>in pairs</u>[2], perform freestyle movements of jumps, spins, lifts, and footwork in a graceful manner. Figure Skating has developed from a practical way to get around on ice into an elegant mix of art and sport today, and is one of the most popular programme of the Olympic Winter Games.

花样滑冰是滑冰运动员单人或双人以跳跃、旋转、托举和步伐组合优美地展示自由滑行动作的一项运动。花样滑冰已经从最早在冰上滑行的方式发展到如今的艺术与运动的完美结合，并成为冬奥会最受欢迎的运动之一。

The Dutch were arguably[3] the earliest pioneers of skating. They began using canals to maintain communication by skating from village to village as far back as the 13th century. Skating eventually spread across the channel to England, and soon the first clubs and artificial rinks began to form.

荷兰人可以说是最早的滑冰先锋。早在 13 世纪，他们就开始利用运河，将滑冰作为村镇间保持联系的交通方式。最终，滑冰穿越海峡传到了英格兰，很快，第一批俱乐部和人造冰场开始出现。

Two Americans are of great importance to its major development in the history of the sport. In 1850, Edward Bushnell of Philadelphia revolutionized skating when he introduced steel-bladed skates allowing complex manoeuvres and turns. Jackson Haines, a ballet master living in Vienna in the 1860s, added elements of ballet and dance to give the sport its grace.

两名美国人对这项运动的发展起到重要作用。1850 年，费城的爱德华·布什内尔引入了钢质冰鞋，使得复杂的动作和转弯得以完成，从而革新了滑冰运动。到 19 世纪 60 年代，住在维也纳的芭蕾舞大师杰克逊·海恩斯为这项运动注入了芭蕾和舞蹈元素，使其增色不少。

Figure Skating is the oldest Olympic Winter Games programme. It was contested at the 1908 London Games and again in 1920 in Antwerp. Men' s, Women' s, and pair' s were the three events contested until 1972. Since 1976, Ice Dance has been the fourth event in the programme, proving a great success.

花样滑冰是冬奥会最古老的运动项目。1908 年伦敦奥运会和 1920 年安特卫普奥运会均包含该项目比赛。直到 1972 年，花样滑冰比赛仅包括男子、女子和双人滑等 3 个小项。自 1976 年以来，冰舞一直是第 4 个小项，并取得了巨大的成功。

The four events of Men' s Singles, Women' s Singles, Pair Skating and Ice Dance are also incorporated into a team event, which appeared for the first time at the 2014 Olympic Winter Games.

男子单人滑、女子单人滑、双人滑和冰舞 4 个项目又组成了花样滑冰的团体赛，并在 2014 年冬奥会首次亮相。

The International Skating Union (ISU) is the governing body for international competitions in Figure Skating, including the World Championships and the Figure Skating events at the Olympic Winter Games.

国际滑冰联盟（ISU）是花样滑冰国际比赛的管理机构，管理世界锦标赛和冬奥会的花样滑冰比赛。

Figure skaters wear leather boots, sometimes custom-fitted[4], reinforced with thick padding to brace the ankle and with wide tongues for control and flexibility. The figure skate' s blade is about 3/16 inch (4.7625 mm) thick. It is hollow-ground[5] to emphasize its two edges, although the skater usually uses only one edge at a time. The front of the blade, called the toe rake, contains serrations[6], which are planted into the ice and help the skater in certain jumps. The blade also allows the skater to pivot quickly

花样滑冰运动员穿着皮制冰鞋，有时是定制的。它用厚实的鞋腰加固，以支撑脚踝，并采用宽舌进行控制，以实现灵活调节。花样滑冰鞋的冰刀厚约 3/16 英寸（4.7625 毫米）。冰刀为双刃，但运动员通常一次只使用一边刀刃。冰刀的前部称为刀齿，上面有锯齿，这些刀齿点在冰上可以帮助运动员做出特定的跳跃动作。冰刀还有助于运动员在冰上

on the ice in order to perform rapid spins. Ice dancers wear skates with shorter blades and looser padding to facilitate quick foot movement.

快速旋转。冰舞运动员的滑冰鞋的冰刀长度较短，鞋腰更矮，鞋垫更松，从而可以方便脚的快速运动。

Vocabulary | 词汇

1.	Figure Skating		花样滑冰
2.	pair	*n.*	一对，一双
3.	arguably [ˈɑːgjuəbli]	*adv.*	可论证地，按理
4.	custom-fitted		适应客户的
5.	hollow-grounded		凹面，凹磨刃
6.	serration [seˈreɪʃn]	*n.*	锯齿边

Language Use | 语言使用

in pairs　　成对的

We worked in pairs for the role-play exercise.

我们两人一组练习角色扮演。

Lesson 4 Ice Hockey

第四课　冰球

Ice Hockey[1] is a fast, fluid[2] and exciting team sport. It draws big crowds at the Olympic Games thanks to the drama and tension of the matches.

Ice Hockey originated in Canada in the early 19th century, based on several similar sports played in Europe, although the word "hockey" came from the old French word "hocquet", meaning "stick". Around 1860, a puck was substituted for a ball, and in 1879 two McGill University students, Robertson and Smith, devised the first rules.

By the late 1800s Ice Hockey competed with lacrosse[3] as Canada' s most popular sport. The first national hockey organisation, the Amateur Hockey Association (AHA) of Canada (which limited players to seven a side), was formed in Montreal in 1885, and the first league was formed in Kingston during the same year, with four teams: the Kingston Hockey Club, Queen' s University, the Kingston Athletics, and the Royal Military College. Queen' s University scored a 3–1 victory over the Athletics in the first championship game.

冰球是一项快速、流畅、激昂的团体运动。由于其戏剧性和紧张性，冰球比赛在冬奥会上吸引了大量观众。

冰球起源于 19 世纪初的加拿大，以欧洲的几种类似运动为基础，但“hockey”一词来自古法语词“hocquet”，意思是“棍子”。1860 年前后，冰球代替了原来的球。1879 年，麦吉尔大学的两名学生罗伯逊和史密斯制定了最早的竞赛规则。

到了 19 世纪后期，冰球已经可以与加拿大最受欢迎的运动曲棍球媲美。1885 年，加拿大第一个国家级冰球组织业余冰球协会（AHA）（将每队球员人数限制为 7 人）在蒙特利尔成立，并于同年在金斯敦组织了第一届联赛，共有 4 支球队参赛：金斯敦冰球俱乐部队、女王大学队、金斯敦竞技队和皇家军事学院队。女王大学队以 3∶1 的比分击败金斯敦竞技队，在第一届联赛中获得冠军。

The sport migrated[4] south to the United States during the 1890s, and games are known to have taken place there between Johns Hopkins University and Yale University in 1895. Ice Hockey spread to Europe around the turn of the century, and the first Olympic Games to include Ice Hockey for men were the 1920 Antwerp Summer Games.

19 世纪 90 年代，冰球运动向南传入美国。1895 年，约翰·霍普金斯大学和耶鲁大学之间举行了多场比赛。冰球在世纪之交传播到了欧洲，1920 年安特卫普夏奥会是第一个纳入男子冰球项目的奥运会。

Six-a-side Men's Ice Hockey has been on the programme of every edition of the Olympic Winter Games since 1924 in Chamonix. Women's Ice Hockey was accepted as an Olympic sport in 1992, and made its official debut in 1998 in Nagano.

自 1924 年夏慕尼冬奥会以来，每一届冬奥会都纳入了六人制男子冰球。1992 年，女子冰球成为奥运项目，并于 1998 年在长野首次正式亮相。

Unsurprisingly, Canada dominated the first tournaments since Ice Hockey was included in the Olympic Winter Games. However, in 1956, and until its dissolution, the Soviet Union took over and became the number one team. It was interrupted only by USA victories in 1960 in Squaw Valley and in 1980 in Lake Placid.

毫无意外，自冰球纳入冬奥会以来，加拿大冰球队一直占据着霸主地位。然而，从 1956 年到苏联解体期间，苏联冰球队在国际比赛中却占有绝对统治地位，成为排名第一的球队，仅在 1960 年斯阔谷冬奥会和 1980 年普莱西德湖冬奥会上被美国队打破了连胜战绩。

Vocabulary | 词汇

1.	Ice Hockey		冰球
2.	fluid [ˈfluːɪd]	*adj.*	流畅的
3.	lacrosse [ləˈkrɒs]	*n.*	长曲棍球
4.	migrate [maɪˈgreɪt]	*v.*	迁徙；移居；迁移

Language Use | 语言使用

take over 接管

Prime candidate to take over his job is Charlie.

接替他工作的首选候选人是查理。

Lesson 5 Curling

第五课　冰壶

Curling[1] is a team sport played by two teams of four players on a rectangular sheet of ice. Its nickname, "the roaring[2] game", originates from the rumbling[3] sound the 44-pound (19.96 kg) granite[4] stones make when they travel across the ice.

As one of the world' s oldest team sports, Curling originated in the 16th century in Scotland, where games were played during winter on frozen ponds and lochs[5]. The earliest-known curling stones came from the Scottish regions of Stirling and Perth and date from 1511. In the 1600s, stones with handles were introduced. The key 20th-century developments in the sport have been the standardisation of the stone, the development of the slide delivery, and the use of indoor, refrigerated[6] ice facilities.

冰壶是一种团体运动，由两支四人队伍在一块长方形冰面上进行比赛。冰壶的绰号为“咆哮游戏”，因为 44 磅（19.96 千克）的花岗岩石冰壶在冰上滑行时会发出隆隆声。

作为世界上最古老的团体运动之一，冰壶起源于 16 世纪的苏格兰，那里的人们冬季在冰冻的池塘和湖泊上进行冰壶比赛。已知最早的冰壶石料来自苏格兰的斯特林和珀斯地区，可追溯至 1511 年。到了 17 世纪，带手柄的冰壶开始出现。进入 20 世纪，这项运动迎来了一系列重要发展，包括石材的标准化、滑行投壶方式的改进及室内冷冻制冰设备的运用。

Curling in its early days was played on frozen lochs and ponds, a pastime[7] still enjoyed in some countries when weather permits; but all national and international competitive Curling competitions now take place in indoor rinks with the condition of the ice carefully temperature-controlled.

It is clear that the first recognised Curling Clubs were formed in Scotland, and during the 19th century the game was exported wherever Scots settled around the world in cold climates, most notably at that time in Canada, USA, Sweden, Switzerland, Norway and New Zealand.

The first rules were drawn up in Scotland, and they were formally adopted as the "Rules in Curling" by the Grand Caledonian Curling Club, which was formed in Edinburgh in 1838 and became the sport' s governing body. Four years later, following a demonstration of Curling on the ballroom floor of Scone Palace near Perth by the Earl of Mansfield during a visit by Queen Victoria, the Queen was so fascinated[8] by the game that in 1843 she gave permission for the Club' s name to be changed to the Royal Caledonian Curling Club (RCCC)–by which it is still known today.

Men' s Curling was included in the Olympic programme in 1924 at the first Olympic Winter Games in Chamonix. It was then dropped, and later re-introduced as a demonstration sport in 1932 in Lake Placid. Between 1936 and 1992, Curling was staged at the Games as a demonstration sport: in Garmisch-Partenkirchen in 1936 and Innsbruck in 1964, and in 1988 in Calgary and in 1992 in Albertville, with both Men' s and Women' s events. It was in Nagano in 1998 that it officially joined the Olympic programme, with both Men' s and Women' s competitions.

早期的冰壶比赛在冰冻的湖泊和池塘上举行。如果天气允许，有些国家仍然喜欢这种消遣活动，但目前所有国际和国家级竞技性冰壶比赛都在室内冰场举行，严格的温度控制保证了冰面的条件。

显然，公认的第一批冰壶俱乐部成立于苏格兰。19 世纪，该运动随着苏格兰人移居全球各地而传到气候寒冷的地方，当时最值得一提的是加拿大、美国、瑞典、瑞士、挪威和新西兰。

最早的竞赛规则在苏格兰制定，大喀里多尼亚冰壶俱乐部正式采纳了这些规则作为“冰壶规则”，该俱乐部于 1838 年在爱丁堡成立，后来成为冰壶运动的管理机构。四年后，在维多利亚女王访问期间，曼斯菲尔德伯爵在珀斯附近的斯康宫舞厅展示了冰壶，女王对冰壶比赛非常着迷，于是在 1843 年，她允许将俱乐部的名称改为皇家喀里多尼亚冰壶俱乐部(RCCC)——这个名称沿用至今。

1924 年，在夏慕尼举行的第一届冬奥会上，男子冰壶被列入奥运项目，随后被取消。之后，在 1932 年普莱西德湖冬奥会上，它作为表演项目重新加入冬奥会。1936 年至 1992 年期间，冰壶作为表演项目出现在 1936 年加米施－帕滕基兴冬奥会、1964 年因斯布鲁克冬奥会、1988 年卡尔加里冬奥会和 1992 年阿尔贝维尔冬奥会上，含男子冰壶和女子冰壶。在 1998 年的长野冬奥会上，冰壶项目的男女比赛均被正式列入了奥运项目。

Vocabulary | 词汇

1. Curling [ˈkɜːlɪŋ] *n.* 冰壶
2. roar [rɔːr] *v.* 咆哮，喧闹，吼叫
3. rumble [ˈrʌmbl] *v.* 隆隆作响
4. granite [ˈɡrænɪt] *n.* 花岗岩，花岗石
5. loch [lɒːk] *n.* 湖，狭长的海湾
6. refrigerate [rɪˈfrɪdʒəreɪt] *v.* 冷藏，冷冻
7. pastime [ˈpɑːstaɪm] *n.* 消遣，娱乐
8. fascinate [ˈfæsɪneɪt] *v.* 使着迷，使神魂颠倒

Language Use | 语言使用

be drawn up 制定

Technical popularisation programme shall be drawn up in popularising agro-techniques.

推广农业技术应当制定农业技术推广项目。

Lesson 6 Cross-Country Skiing

第六课　越野滑雪

Cross-Country Skiing is the oldest type of skiing. It emerged from a need to travel over snow-covered terrain[1] and developed into a sport at the end of the 19th century.

越野滑雪是最古老的滑雪类型，源于人们在积雪覆盖的地面上行走的需要，后于 19 世纪末发展成为一项运动。

For centuries in the snow-covered North, skis were required to chase[2] game and gather firewood in wintertime. With long distances between the small, isolated communities, skiing also became important as a means of keeping in social contact. The word "ski" is a Norwegian word which comes from the Norse word "skid".

几个世纪以来，在积雪覆盖的北方，人们一到冬季就会使用滑雪板追逐猎物或者采集木柴。由于独立的小社区之间距离较远，滑雪也成为保持社会联系的重要手段。"ski"（滑雪）一词源自挪威语词语"skid"。

Different types of skis emerged at various regions at about the same time. The modern ski bindings are based on the Fennoscandian[3] model of the 19th century. The East Siberian type was a thin board with a vertical four-hole binding. Sometimes it was covered with fur. The Lapps[4] used a horizontal stem-hole binding. Present-day Cross-Country skis were developed from the type used by the Lapps.

几乎在同一时间，在不同地区出现了不同类型的滑雪板。现代滑雪板固定器源于 19 世纪的芬诺斯堪迪亚地区的模型。东西伯利亚滑雪板则是一块薄板，通过垂直的四孔固定，有时还会覆有动物毛皮。拉普兰人使用水平杆孔固定。现在的越野滑雪板是以拉普兰人所使用的类型为基础开发的。

Skiing for sport appeared in Norway in the mid-19th century; the first race on record was in 1842. The famous Holmenkollen Ski Festival started in 1892, with the focus initially on the Nordic Combined event. However, in 1901, a separate Cross-Country race was added to the festival.

19世纪中期，挪威出现了体育滑雪比赛；有记载的第一场比赛于1842年举行。1892年，著名的霍尔门科伦滑雪节开始举办，最初只举行北欧两项赛事。之后在1901年，滑雪节增加了单独的越野滑雪比赛。

The Men’s event debuted at the first Olympic Winter Games in Chamonix in 1924 and the Women’s event debuted at the 1952 Oslo Games. The sport has traditionally been dominated by the Nordic countries.

越野滑雪的男子赛事于1924年在夏慕尼冬奥会上首次亮相，女子赛事在1952年的奥斯陆冬奥会上首次亮相。北欧国家在该项目上占据统治地位。

The Cross-Country Skiing competition consists of 12 different Cross-Country Skiing events. Women compete in the sprint, team sprint, 10 km individual start, 15 km pursuit, 30 km mass start and the 4×5 km relay. Men compete in the sprint, team sprint, 15 km individual start, 30 km pursuit, 50 km mass start and the 4×10 km relay.

越野滑雪比赛包括12个小项。女子项目包括短距离、团体短距离、10公里个人出发、15公里双追逐，30公里集体出发和4×5公里接力。男子项目包括短距离、团体短距离、15公里个人出发、30公里双追逐、50公里集体出发和4×10公里接力。

Vocabulary | 词汇

1. terrain [tə'reɪn] *n.* 地形，地势，地面
2. chase [tʃeɪs] *v.* 追逐，追赶
3. Fennoscandian *adj.* 芬诺斯堪迪亚地区的
4. Lapps [læps] *n.* 拉普兰人

Language Use | 语言使用

as a means of 作为……的手段

Trade should not serve as a means of economic plunder.

贸易不应当成为经济掠夺的手段。

Lesson 7 Ski Jumping

第七课　跳台滑雪

Ski Jumping[1] is a winter sport in which competitors aim to achieve the longest jump after descending[2] from a specially designed ramp[3] on their skis. Along with jump length, competitor' s style and other factors affect the final score. Ski Jumping was first contested in Norway in the late 19th century, and later spread through Europe and North America in the early 20th century. Along with Cross-Country Skiing, it constitutes the traditional group of Nordic skiing disciplines.

Like most of the Nordic skiing disciplines, the first Ski Jumping competitions were held in Norway in the 19th century, although there was evidence of Ski Jumping in the late 18th century. The origin of Ski Jumping can be traced to Ole Rye who jumped 9.5m in 1808. Norwegian Sondre Norheim is widely considered the father of modern Ski Jumping. In 1866, he won

跳台滑雪是一项冬季运动项目，选手们脚踏滑雪板从专门设计的坡道往下跳跃，争取赢得最长的跳跃距离。除了跳跃距离，选手的风格和其他因素也会影响最终得分。19 世纪后期，跳台滑雪比赛首次在挪威出现，20 世纪初传遍了欧洲和北美洲。跳台滑雪和越野滑雪都属于传统的北欧滑雪项目。

虽有证据表明，跳台滑雪在 18 世纪晚期就已经出现，但与大多数北欧滑雪项目类似，其最早的赛事于 19 世纪在挪威举行。跳台滑雪可以追溯到 1808 年，当时奥莱·莱依跳跃了 9.5 米。挪威人森德·诺海姆是公认的现代跳台滑雪之父。1866 年，他于在挪威举办的世界上

what has been described as the world' s first Ski Jumping competition with prizes, held in Norway. The first larger Ski Jumping competition was held in Oslo, Norway, in 1875. Due to its poor infrastructure and the weather conditions, in 1892 the event was moved to Holmenkollen, which is today still one of the main Ski Jumping events in the season.

第一场设立奖项的跳台滑雪比赛中胜出。1875 年，在挪威奥斯陆首次举办了较大规模的跳台滑雪比赛。由于基础设施和天气状况不佳，1892 年，该赛事移至霍尔门科伦举行，直到今天它仍然是主要的冬季跳台滑雪赛事之一。

After World War I, Thulin Thams and Sigmund Ruud developed a new jumping style known as the Kongsberger Technique. This involved jumping with the upper body bent at the hips, a wide forward lean, and with arms extended at the front with the skis parallel[4] to each other. Using this technique Sepp Bradl of Austria became the first to jump more than 100 metres when he jumped 101 metres in 1936. In the mid-1950s, Swiss jumper Andreas Daescher became the first jumper to hold the arms backwards close to the body with a more extreme forward lean. Then in 1985, Swedish jumper Jan Bokloev started spreading the tips of his skis into a "V" shape. Initially ridiculed[5], this technique proved so successful that by 1992 all Olympic medallists were using this style.

第一次世界大战后，图灵·萨马思和希哥穆德·汝德发明了一种名为“空斯伯格技术”的新型跳跃方式，即上半身弯曲，身体前倾，双臂向前方伸展，滑雪板彼此平行。依靠这种技术，奥地利的塞普·布拉德尔在 1936 年跳出了 101 米，成为第一个跳 100 米以上的选手。20 世纪 50 年代中期，瑞士选手安德烈亚斯·戴舍尔率先采用了双臂向后靠近身体、前倾角度更大的方式。之后在 1985 年，瑞典选手简·波克勒夫开始将滑雪板的顶端打开分成“V”形。虽然该技术最初遭到嘲笑，但事实证明它非常成功，到了 1992 年，所有获得奥运奖牌的选手都使用了这种技术。

Ski Jumping was brought to Canada by Norwegian immigrant Nels Nelsen. Starting with his example in 1915 until the late 1960s, annual Ski Jumping competitions were held on Mount Revelstoke–the ski hill Nelsen designed–the most time-honoured Ski Jumping venue in Canada. Revelstoke' s was the biggest natural ski jump hill in Canada and internationally recognised as one of the best in North America. The length and natural grade of its 600m hill made possible jumps of over 60 metres–the longest in Canada.

挪威移民尼尔斯·尼尔森将跳台滑雪带到了加拿大。从他在 1915 年的示范开始，直到 20 世纪 60 年代后期，在他设计的滑雪场地——雷夫尔斯托克跳台每年都举行比赛，这是加拿大历史最悠久的跳台滑雪场地。雷夫尔斯托克还是加拿大最大的天然跳台滑雪场，也是国际公认的北美最佳滑雪场之一。其 600 米山坡形成的长度和坡度可以让人跳出 60 米以上的距离，也是加拿大最远距离。

Ski Jumping has been part of the Olympic Winter Games since the first Games in Chamonix in 1924. The normal hill competition was included in the Olympic programme for the 1964 Innsbruck Games.

自 1924 年夏慕尼首届冬奥会以来，跳台滑雪一直是冬奥会的项目之一。1964 年因斯布鲁克冬奥会还加入了标准台的比赛。

Vocabulary | 词汇

1.	Ski Jumping		跳台滑雪
2.	descend [dɪˈsend]	*v.*	下来，下降
3.	ramp [ræmp]	*n.*	斜坡；斜道
4.	parallel [ˈpærəlel]	*adj.*	平行的；相同的
5.	ridicule [ˈrɪdɪkjuːl]	*v.*	嘲笑

Language Use | 语言使用

along with 和……一起

Along with the award, the winners also got a free trip to New York City.

除了奖品以外，获胜者还得到去纽约免费旅行的机会。

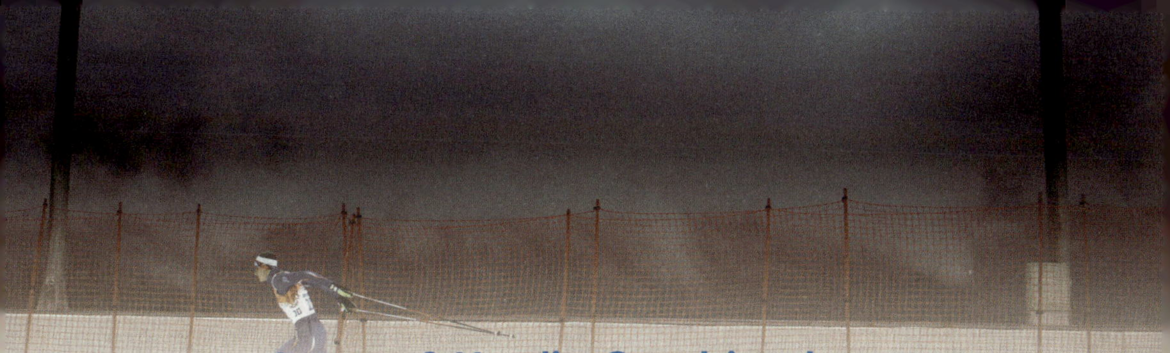

Lesson 8 Nordic Combined

第八课　北欧两项

Nordic Combined[1], as the name implies, combines the two main elements of Nordic skiing: Cross-Country Skiing and Ski Jumping. Originally, it was a 90-metre jump followed by 15km of skiing. Today, there are several varieties. Nordic Combined has been called the "decathlon[2] of skiing" because it requires a skier to use two totally opposite muscle groups–explosiveness[3] and strength for takeoff in Ski Jumping, then swiftness and endurance for Cross-Country.

Today, Nordic Combined is a very popular sport in <u>a number of</u> countries, in Scandinavian Countries, Japan, Germany, Russia, France and Austria. The International Ski Federation(FIS) conducts regular World Cup events, and every second year a FIS World Championships is held. After introducing the SPRINT event–a single-day short event–FIS was able to attract more spectators and gain better television ratings.

The Nordic Combined events have been on the Olympic programme since the first Winter Games in Chamonix, France, and for the first 12 years, Norwegians won every available medal. In those pre-war years, the Nordic Combined gold medallist was often a top athlete for Cross-Country Skiing and Ski Jumping as well.

Finland and Sweden broke up Norway' s dominance[4] in this sport immediately after World War II, but the modern age really began in 1960 when a German, Georg Thoma,

顾名思义，北欧两项结合了北欧滑雪的两大要素：越野滑雪和跳台滑雪。最初的比赛形式是 90 米跳台滑雪和 15 公里越野滑雪，现在发展成为好几种形式。北欧两项被称为“滑雪中的十项全能”，因为它要求滑雪选手使用两种完全相反的肌肉群的力量——跳台滑雪的爆发力和起跳力，以及越野滑雪的灵敏性和耐力。

如今，北欧两项在斯堪的纳维亚国家、日本、德国、俄罗斯、法国和奥地利等许多国家都很盛行。国际滑雪联合会（简称“国际雪联”）定期举办世界杯赛事，并且每两年举办一次世界锦标赛。在引入了短距离项目（一个为期一天的短项目）之后，国际雪联吸引了更多观众，并取得了更高的电视节目收视率。

北欧两项自法国夏慕尼第一届冬奥会就一直是奥运项目，在冬奥会举办的前 12 年间，挪威人包揽了所有北欧两项的奖牌。在第二次世界大战之前，北欧两项金牌得主通常也是顶尖单项运动员。

芬兰和瑞典在第二次世界大战后迅速打破了挪威在北欧两项中的主导地位，1960 年德国人乔治·托马成为该项目获

became the first non-Scandinavian to win in Nordic Combined. The German Democratic Republic' s Ulrich Wehling captured three gold medals from 1972–1980, becoming the first three-time winner of a particular Nordic skiing event.

胜的第一个非斯堪的纳维亚人时，北欧两项才开始真正进入现代时期。民主德国的乌尔里希·韦林从 1972 年到 1980 年间获得 3 枚金牌，成为第一个北欧滑雪项目的三连冠选手。

The Chinese Nordic Combined national teams were officially established in November 2017 and went to Finland for training for the first time on 20 January 2018. After nearly one year' s training, it has achieved initial results with active participation of Continental Cup and Nordic Championship during 2018–2019 and 2019–2020 seasons, which lay a good foundation for World Cup competitions.

中国北欧两项国家队于 2017 年 11 月正式组建，在 2018 年 1 月 20 日首次赴芬兰外训。在经过近一年外训后初见成效，于 2018—2019 赛季和 2019—2020 赛季参加洲际杯和北欧世锦赛，为之后世界杯参赛打下坚实基础。

Vocabulary | 词汇

1.	Nordic Combined		北欧两项
2.	decathlon [dɪˈkæθlən]	*n.*	滑雪中的十项全能
3.	explosiveness [ɪksp'loʊsɪvnəs]	*n.*	爆发力
4.	dominance ['dɒmɪnəns]	*n.*	统治

Language Use | 语言使用

1. a number of　　许多的；大量的

   In her haste to complete the work on time, she made a number of mistakes.

   她急急忙忙想按时完工，结果出了不少错。

2. lay a good foundation for　　为……打下良好基础

   A positive learning attitude can not only improve the quality of study but also lay a good foundation for lifelong learning.

   积极的学习态度不仅能提高学习的质量，而且能为终身学习打下良好的基础。

Lesson 9 Alpine Skiing

第九课　高山滑雪

Alpine Skiing[1] is the sport activity of sliding down snow-covered slopes on skis with fixed-heel bindings, unlike other types of skiing (Cross-Country Skiing or Ski Jumping), which use skis with free-heel bindings. Modern competitive Alpine Skiing is divided into the so-called speed and technical events, the former comprising Downhill and the Super Giant Slalom, or Super-G, and the latter including the Slalom and Giant Slalom. The speed events are contested in single runs down long, steep, fast courses featuring few turns and widely spread gates. The technical events challenge the skier' s ability to manoeuvre over courses marked by closely spaced gates through which both skis must pass simultaneously; winners are determined by the lowest combined time in two runs on two different courses. The Alpine Combined events consist of a Downhill and a Slalom race, with the winner having the lowest combined time. FIS is the worldwide governing body of the sport.

高山滑雪是一种利用带有脚跟固定装置的滑雪板在雪道中由上向下滑的体育活动。其他滑雪项目（越野滑雪或跳台滑雪）使用的固定装置在脚跟处与雪板可以实现分离。现代竞技性高山滑雪分为速度项目和技术项目。前者包括滑降和超级大回转，后者包括回转和大回转。速度项目采用单轮制，赛道较长且陡峭，滑行速度快，转弯较少，且旗门间距较大。技术项目则挑战运动员在间距较近旗门的赛道上展示滑行技术的能力，两块滑雪板必须一起通过这些旗门。在同一赛道（两次线路不同）上进行两轮滑行后，综合时间最短的运动员获胜。高山滑雪全能项目包括了滑降或回转，综合时间最短的运动员获胜。国际雪联是这项运动的全球管理机构。

Skiing has an ancient history. The birth of modern Downhill is often dated to the 1850s when Norwegian legend Sondre Norheim popularised skis with curved slides and stiff heel bindings made of willow[2], as well as the Christiania (slalom) turns.

滑雪运动历史悠久。现代滑降通常可以追溯到 19 世纪 50 年代，当时挪威的传奇人物桑德・诺尔海姆推广了具有弯曲面、采用柳树制成的坚硬脚跟固定装置的滑雪板和克里斯蒂安尼亚（回转）弯道。

Skiing can be traced to prehistoric times by the discovery of varying sizes and shapes of wooden planks preserved in peat bogs in Russia, Finland, Sweden and Norway. Ski fragments discovered in Russia have been carbon-dated back to circa 8000 – 7000 BC. It is virtually[3] certain that a form of skiing has been an integral part of people' s life in colder countries for thousands of years.

根据在俄罗斯、芬兰、瑞典和挪威发现的在泥炭沼泽中保存的大小不一的木板形状，可以将滑雪运动追溯到史前时期。根据放射性碳素断代法，在俄罗斯发现的滑雪板碎片可以追溯到公元前 8000 年到公元前 7000 年。几乎可以肯定，几千年来，某种形式的滑雪一直是气候寒冷的国家中人民生活中不可或缺的一部分。

Skiing was changed from a method of transport into a sport during the late 19th century. The first non-military skiing competitions are reported to have been held in the 1840s in northern and central Norway. The first national skiing competition in Norway, held in the capital Christiania (now Oslo) and won by Sondre Norheim, in 1868, is regarded as the beginning of a new era of skiing enthusiasm. A few decades later, the sport spread to other parts of Europe and to the U.S., where miners held skiing competitions to entertain themselves during the winter. The first Slalom competition was organised by Sir Arnold Lunn in 1922 in Mürren, Switzerland.

19 世纪后期，滑雪从交通方式转变为体育活动。据说，19 世纪 40 年代挪威中北部举行了第一场非军事滑雪比赛。1868 年，挪威首场全国性滑雪比赛在首都克里斯蒂安尼亚（现在的奥斯陆）举行，被公认开启了滑雪风靡的新时代，当时桑德・诺尔海姆获得了冠军。几十年后，这项运动传播到了欧洲其他地区和美国，当地的矿工们在冬季举行滑雪比赛作为娱乐。1922 年，阿诺德・伦恩爵士在瑞士米伦组织了第一场回转滑雪比赛。

Men' s and Women' s Alpine Skiing both debuted on the Olympic programme in 1936 at Garmisch-Partenkirchen. The only event that year was a combined competition of both Downhill and Slalom. In 1948, this was held along with separate Downhill and Slalom races. Four years later, the Giant Slalom was added and in 1988 the Super Giant Slalom became a fourth separate event.

在 1936 年加米施-帕滕基兴冬奥会上，男子和女子高山滑雪首次加入奥运项目。当时只设置了一个项目，即滑降和回转综合比赛。1948 年，又举行了单独的滑降比赛和回转比赛。四年后，又增加了大回转比赛，1988 年，超级大回转成为第 4 个独立小项。

Vocabulary | 词汇

1. Alpine Skiing 高山滑雪
2. willow [ˈwɪləʊ] *n.* 柳树
3. virtually [ˈvɜːtʃuəli] *adv.* 事实上

Language Use | 语言使用

be changed from...into... 从……转变为……

Summer' s topic has changed from enjoyment into suffering.

夏日的主题已经从欢乐转变成煎熬了。

Lesson 10 Freestyle Skiing

第十课　自由式滑雪

Freestyle Skiing is a skiing discipline that includes Aerials[1], Moguls[2], Ski Cross[3], Half-pipe[4], Slopestyle[5] and Big Air[6] as part of the Olympic Winter Games. It is also commonly referred to as freeski, jibbing, as well as many other names around the world.

Freestyle Skiing combines speed, showmanship[7] and the ability to perform aerial manoeuvres whilst skiing. There were records of people performing somersaults[8] on skis at the beginning of the 20th century in Norway, Italy and Austria, and in the early 1920s, the U.S. skiers started to flip and spin.

自由式滑雪是冬奥会的滑雪项目之一，包括空中技巧、雪上技巧、障碍追逐、U 型场地技巧、坡面障碍技巧和大跳台。在世界各地，自由式滑雪有自由滑雪、障碍技巧滑雪等多种名称。

自由式滑雪结合了速度、表现力和滑雪过程中的空中动作控制能力。据记载，20 世纪初，在挪威、意大利和奥地利，已经有人穿着滑雪板空翻，到 20 世纪 20 年代早期，美国的滑雪选手们开始了空翻和旋转。

Aerials and moguls were popularised in the 1950s by Olympic gold medallist Stein Eriksen. Freestyle Skiing really began to take off in America during the 1960s when social change and freedom of expression together with the advances in ski equipment led to the new and exciting development of skiing techniques. Freestyle Skiing was affectionately known as "hotdogging". The name seemed to perfectly capture the breath-taking mix of acrobatic tricks, jumps and sheer[9] adrenalin[10] rush of the sport. Freestyle Skiing was recognised as a discipline by the FIS in 1979. The governing body brought in new regulations in an effort to curb some of the dangerous elements of the new and developing sport and the first FIS World Cup series was staged the following year.

20 世纪 50 年代，奥运会金牌得主斯坦・埃里克森推广了技巧滑雪。20 世纪 60 年代，自由式滑雪真正开始在美国得到发展，当时的社会改革、言论自由及滑雪设备的进步带来了令人兴奋的滑雪新技术发展。自由式滑雪被亲切地称为"hotdogging"（卖弄技巧）。这个名字似乎完美体现了这项运动的杂技技巧、跳跃和纯粹的肾上腺素刺激的惊人结合。1979 年，自由式滑雪作为一个分项被纳入国际雪联大家庭。作为该项运动的管理机构，国际雪联引入了新的条例，减少这项新兴运动中的一些危险元素。次年，第一届国际雪联世界杯系列赛成功举办。

The first FIS Freestyle Ski World Cup was staged in 1980 and the first FIS Freestyle World Ski Championships took place in 1986 in Tignes, France. Freestyle Skiing was contested as an exhibition event sport at the 1988 Calgary Games. There were three events for both men and women–Moguls, Aerials and Ballet. Four years later, moguls gained medal status at the Albertville Games, as did Aerials in Lillehammer in 1994. Ski Cross made its Olympic debut at the 2010 Vancouver Games. Slopestyle and Halfpipe were added to the Freestyle Skiing programme at the 2014 Sochi Games. Big Air was contested for the first time at the 2019 FIS World Championships and will make its Olympic debut in the Olympic Winter Games Beijing 2022.

第一届国际雪联自由式滑雪世界杯于 1980 年登场，而第一届国际雪联自由式滑雪世锦赛于 1986 年在法国蒂涅举行。在 1988 年卡尔加里冬奥会上，自由式滑雪被列为表演项目。男女项目各设 3 个小项：雪上技巧、空中技巧和雪上芭蕾。四年后，在阿尔贝维尔冬奥会上，雪上技巧项目成为正式比赛项目。在 1994 年的利勒哈默尔冬奥会上，空中技巧成为正式比赛项目。障碍追逐项目在 2010 年温哥华冬奥会上正式亮相。坡面障碍技巧和 U 形场地技巧成为 2014 年索契冬奥会的自由式滑雪比赛项目。2019 年，大跳台项目第一次成为国际雪联世界锦标赛正式比赛项目，并将在 2022 年北京冬奥会上奉献奥运项目首秀。

Vocabulary | 词汇

1. Aerials [ˈeəriəls]	*n.*	空中技巧
2. Moguls [ˈməʊgls]	*n.*	雪上技巧
3. Ski Cross		障碍追逐
4. Halfpipe		U 型场地技巧
5. Slopestyle [ˌsləʊpˈstaɪl]	*n.*	坡面障碍技巧
6. Big Air		大跳台
7. showmanship [ˈʃəʊmənʃɪp]	*n.*	表现力
8. somersault [ˈsʌməsɔːlt]	*n.*	跟斗，颠倒，空翻
9. sheer [ʃɪər]	*adj.*	纯粹的，仅仅的
10. adrenalin [əˈdrenəlɪn]	*n.*	肾上腺素

Language Use | 语言使用

in an effort to　　企图，努力想

They hushed up the scandal in an effort to avoid further damages.

他们掩盖了丑闻以避免进一步损失。

Lesson 11 Snowboard

第十一课　单板滑雪

Snowboard[1] is a winter sport stemming from skiing, surfing and skateboard, where the primary activity is descending a snow-covered slope while standing on a snowboard with feet positioned roughly perpendicular to the board and its moving direction, further differentiating it from skiing, in which riders face forward. Moreover, no poles are used in Snowboard, and the majority of participants wear not hard but soft to medium flex boots for support. The sport is governed by the FIS.

Snowboard was developed in the United States in the 1960s as people across the U.S began to seek out new winter activities. Over the next decade, various pioneers boosted the production of boards and the sport began to gain crossover appeal. Surfers[2] and skateboarders[3] became involved, and by 1980, Snowboard was a nationwide activity.

单板滑雪是在滑雪、冲浪和滑板运动基础上发展起来的冬季运动，运动员站在一块滑雪板上从雪坡上向下滑行，双脚大致与滑雪板和前进方向垂直。与双板滑雪的不同之处在于，单板滑雪选手面朝前方。此外，单板滑雪不使用雪杖，并且大多数人不穿硬靴，而穿柔软至中度弯曲的靴子用于支撑。单板滑雪运动由国际雪联管理。

20 世纪 60 年代，美国人开始探寻新的冬季活动，单板滑雪运动由此兴起。接下来的十年里，单板滑雪的先驱们提高了滑雪板的产量，这项运动获得了广泛的吸引力。喜欢冲浪和玩滑板的人也开始玩单板滑雪，到了 1980 年，单板滑雪已经成为全国性运动。

In the late 1970s snowboarders started to "invade" traditional ski resorts, but faced opposition from skiers who tried to exclude the snowboarders from "their" mountains. By the 1990s, however, almost all ski resorts had accepted Snowboard, and the resorts have found the snowboarders to be an excellent source of new revenue.

到了20世纪70年代后期，单板滑雪爱好者开始“入侵”传统的滑雪场，但遭到滑雪者的反对，他们试图将玩单板滑雪的人赶出“他们的”地盘。但到了20世纪90年代，几乎所有滑雪场都接受了单板滑雪，因为它们发现单板滑雪是一个很好的新的收入来源。

Competition was the next logical step. The United States held its first National Championships in 1982 and hosted the first World Championships in 1983. The International Snowboard Federation (ISF) was founded seven years later and the FIS introduced Snowboard as a FIS discipline in 1994. This helped pave the way for Snowboard' s inclusion in the Olympic Winter Games.

比赛自然而然地随之出现。1982年，美国举行了第一届全国锦标赛，并于1983年举办了第一届世界锦标赛。七年后，国际单板滑雪联合会（ISF）正式成立，1994年国际雪联将单板滑雪列为国际雪联项目，为单板滑雪进入冬奥会铺平了道路。

Men' s and Women' s Snowboard made their Olympic debuts at the Nagano Games in 1998 with Giant Slalom and Halfpipe competitions. The discipline proved an instant success and returned to Salt Lake City four years later with Parallel Giant Slalom and Halfpipe competitions. In Turin, Snowboard Cross also made its debut. In this event, four riders race across a course studded with jumps, bumps and huge turns.

在1998年长野冬奥会上，男子和女子单板滑雪（包括大回转和U型场地技巧项目）首次登上奥运会的舞台。该项目大获成功，并在四年后带着平行大回转和U型场地技巧项目再次出现在盐湖城冬奥会上。在都灵冬奥会上，单板滑雪障碍追逐项目首次亮相。这个小项的比赛方式是四名选手在一个布满障碍、缓冲块和大转弯的赛道上互相追逐。

The Snowboard events in the Beijing 2022 Games include Big Air, Halfpipe, Parallel Giant Slalom[4], Snowboard Cross[5] for both men and women.

2022年北京冬奥会的单板滑雪小项包括男女大跳台、U形场地技巧、平行大回转和单板滑雪障碍追逐。

Vocabulary | 词汇

1.	Snowboard [ˈsnəʊbɔːdɪŋ]	*n.*	单板滑雪
2.	surfer [ˈsɜːfər]	*n.*	冲浪运动员，冲浪者
3.	skateboarder [skeɪtbɔːdə]	*n.*	滑板运动员，玩滑板的人
4.	Parallel Giant Slalom		平行大回转
5.	Snowboard Cross		单板滑雪障碍追逐

Language Use | 语言使用

differentiate... from... 将……与……区别开来

A child may not differentiate his/her imagination from the real world.

儿童可能无法将自己的幻想与真实世界区分开来。

Lesson 12 Biathlon

第十二课　冬季两项

The word biathlon[1] stems from the Greek word for two contests, and is today seen as the joining of two sports: skiing and shooting. Biathlon has its roots in survival skills practised in the snow-covered forests of Scandinavia, where people hunted on skis with rifles slung[2] over their shoulders.

冬季两项这个词来源于希腊语，意思是两个比赛。现今该词指滑雪和射击两种体育项目的结合。冬季两项运动起源于在斯堪的那维亚大雪覆盖的森林中（人们）的生存技能，在那里人们把步枪悬挂在肩膀上进行滑雪和狩猎。

In 1948, the Union Internationale de Pentathlon Moderne et Biathlon (UIPMB) was founded, to standardise the rules for Biathlon and Pentathlon[3]. In 1993, the Biathlon branch of the UIPMB created the International Biathlon Union (IBU), which officially separated from the UIPMB in 1998.

1948 年，国际现代五项和冬季两项联合会（UIPMB）成立，开始为冬季两项和五项全能运动制定标准化的规则。UIPMB 的冬季两项分会于 1993 年成立了国际冬季两项联盟（IBU），该联盟于 1998 年正式脱离 UIPMB。

In 1924 in Chamonix, an ancient form of Biathlon made its Olympic debut: the military patrol[4]. This event was then in

1924 年，在夏慕尼，古老形式的冬季两项以“军事巡逻”的形式在奥运会上首次亮相，并在此后的 1928 年、1936

demonstration in 1928, 1936 and 1948. After some attempts to be incorporated into a winter Pentathlon, Biathlon appeared at the Games in its current form in 1960 in Squaw Valley. Women' s Biathlon made its first appearance on the Olympic Winter Games in Albertville in 1992.

Until the Innsbruck 1976 Games, the events comprised an individual race and a relay. In Lake Placid in 1980, a second individual event was introduced.

In Salt Lake City in 2002, a 12.5 km Pursuit event was added for men and 10 km for women. In Turin in 2006, a new Mass Start event was introduced for both men and women. This brings together the 30 best athletes from the World Cup.

年和 1948 年奥运会上得到展示。在几次被试图纳入冬季五项全能运动后，冬季两项于 1960 年在斯阔谷以目前的形式现身冬奥会。女子冬季两项比赛于 1992 年在阿尔贝维尔举行的冬奥会上首次亮相。

直到 1976 年因斯布鲁克冬奥会，冬季两项赛事一直由一项个人赛和一项接力赛组成。1980 年的普莱西德湖冬奥会才引入了第二项个人赛事。

2002 年盐湖城冬奥会增加了男子 12.5 公里、女子 10 公里追逐比赛。2006 年都灵冬奥会引入了一项新的男女集体出发项目。它汇集了来自世界杯的 30 位最佳运动员。

Vocabulary | 词汇

1. Biathlon [baɪˈæθlən]	*n.*	冬季两项
2. slung [slʌŋ]	*v.*	挂；吊（sling 的过去式）
3. Pentathlon [penˈtæθlən]	*n.*	五项全能运动
4. patrol [pəˈtroʊl]	*n.*	巡逻

Language Use | 语言使用

1. stem from　出于，基于

   Correct decisions stem from correct judgments.

   正确的决策源自正确的判断。

2. separate from　分开，脱钩

   After twelve years, he decided to separate from the firm.

   12 年后他决定离开这个公司。

Lesson 13 Bobsleigh
第十三课　雪车

Bobsleigh[1] is a winter sport in which teams of two or four members (with the exception of the newly added event of Women' s Monobob) make timed runs down narrow, twisting, banked, iced tracks in a gravity-powered sleigh. The times for all the runs are added up to calculate the final score. The international competitions and their organisation are governed by the International Bobsleigh and Skeleton Federation (IBSF).

Except for the Women' s Monobob, Bobsleigh events are all team sport in which a crew of either two or four people push and ride down an ice track with the fastest team making it to the finish line crowned[2] the winners. At the start, teams push the sled as fast as they can and then jump into the Bobsleigh in quick succession. It takes balance and agility for up to four powerful athletes to load a sled whilst pushing at maximum velocity[3].

雪车项目作为一项冬季运动，是由两名或四名运动员组成的队伍（新增加的女子单人项目除外）利用重力驱动的雪车在狭窄、弯曲、倾斜和人工制冰的轨道上进行计时竞赛，计时结果相加即得出总成绩。雪车项目的国际竞赛与组织由国际雪车联合会管理。

除了女子单人雪车小项外，雪车项目都是团体运动项目，由两人或四人小组推动雪车并沿着冰道滑行，用时最短到达终点线的队伍获胜。比赛开始时，队员们以最快的速度推动并相继快速跳上雪车。最多四名强壮的运动员需要以最大速度推动雪车后跳上雪车，这需要出色的平衡能力和灵活性。

After the start the pilot[4] takes over the steering[5] and navigates the bobsleigh through a sequence of tricky[6] turns reaching a speed of up to 150 km/h. When the bobsleigh reaches the finish line, the brake person[7] slows the sled down to a stop.

起动后，舵手负责掌舵，操作雪车通过一系列复杂的转弯，速度最高可达150千米每时。雪车通过终点线后，刹车手将雪车减速至停车。

By the 1950s, the critical importance of the start had been recognised and athletes with explosive strength from other sports were drawn to Bobsleigh. In 1952, a critical rule change limiting the total weight of crew and sled ended the era of the super heavyweight Bobsleigh athletes.

到20世纪50年代，由于认识到起跑的重要性，来自其他运动项目具有爆发力的运动员加入了雪车项目。1952年，限制运动员和雪车总重量的重要规则改革结束了超重量级雪车运动员的时代。

In the beginning, the sleds were made of wood. However, they were soon replaced by steel sleds that came to be known as bobsleighs because of the way crews bobbed back and forth to increase their speed at the start. Today, the world' s top teams train and compete mostly on artificial ice tracks in sleek high-tech sleds made of fibreglass[8] and steel.

最初的比赛使用的是由木头制成骨架的雪车，但很快被后来大家所熟知的钢制骨架雪车取代，由于运动员在起跑时前后晃动，因此雪车的英文名叫作bobsleigh。如今，世界顶级团队主要利用由玻璃纤维和钢制成的造型优美的高科技雪车在人造冰道训练和比赛。

Bobsleigh teams include a brake person and a pilot in the two-person, while two crew members/pushers are added for the four-person race. From a standing start, the crew pushes the sled in unison up to 50 metres. This distance is typically covered in less than six seconds when the bobsled will reach a speed of over 40 km/h before the crew loads the sled.

在双人赛中，车队包括一名刹车手和一名舵手，四人赛则增加两名队员或推车员。队员们在起点站立，出发后一起将雪车推出最多50米，一般是在6秒内推完50米，速度达到40千米每时，之后队员们进入雪车就座。

Race times are recorded in hundredths of seconds, so even seemingly[9] minor errors–especially those at the beginning, which affect the remainder of the heat–can have an immeasurable impact on the final race standings.

比赛计时以百分之一秒为单位，因此即使是看似微不足道的失误——尤其是起跑时的失误会影响后期动能——也会对最终的比赛结果产生相当大的影响。

Vocabulary | 词汇

1. Bobsleigh [ˈbɒbsleɪ] *n.* 雪车，有舵雪橇
2. crown [kraʊn] *v.* 给……以荣誉
3. velocity [vəˈlɒsəti] *n.* 速度
4. pilot [ˈpaɪlət] *n.* 舵手，驾驶员
5. steer [stɪər] *v.* 驾驶，操纵
6. tricky [ˈtrɪki] *adj.* 复杂的，微妙的
7. brake person 制动员，刹车手
8. fibreglass [ˈfaɪbəglɑːs] *n.* 玻璃纤维
9. seemingly [ˈsiːmɪŋli] *adv.* 看来似乎，表面上看来

Language Use | 语言使用

1. in succession 接着，接连地

   He hit three bull' s eyes in succession.

   他连续 3 次射中靶心。

2. a sequence of 一系列的

   He had to attend a sequence of meetings.

   他得参加一系列会议。

Lesson 14 Skeleton

第十四课　钢架雪车

Skeleton[1] is a discipline of the Olympic Winter Games where the competitor rides head-first and prone[2] (lying face down) on a flat skeleton sled. It normally runs on an ice track that allows the skeleton to gain speed by gravity. It is considered the world' s first sliding sport. The sport is similar to, but not to be confused with Luge, another form of sled racing where the competitor rides on the back and feet-first. Although sharing the same courses in most cases, the two disciplines have different racing physics. The international Skeleton events and their organisation are governed by the International Bobsleigh and Skeleton Federation (IBSF).

Sleighing is one of the oldest winter sports. Descriptions of the sport can be found in 16th-century literature, but as a racing sport it can be traced to the mid-19th century, when British tourists started sliding down snowbound roads in the Alps. British and American holidaymakers built the first toboggan run in Davos in 1882.

钢架雪车是冬奥会项目，运动员头朝前俯卧趴在平坦的橇上。通常在冰道上滑行，以便使钢架雪车通过重力获得速度。钢架雪车被认为是世界上第一个滑行运动项目。这项运动与雪橇类似，但也不能混为一谈。雪橇是另一种形式的滑行运动项目，运动员脚朝前而背躺在雪橇上。虽然通常使用相同的赛道，但其中所包含的运动物理学原理并不完全一致。钢架雪车项目的国际竞赛与组织由国际雪车联合会（IBSF）管理。

雪橇运动是最古老的冬季运动之一。关于这项运动的描述曾在16世纪的文献中出现，但作为一项竞速运动可以追溯到19世纪中叶，当时英国游客开始在阿尔卑斯山大雪覆盖的道路上滑行。1882年，英国和美国的度假观光旅客在达沃斯建造了第一条滑道。

It was first contested at the 1928 Olympic Winter Games in St. Moritz and again in the 1948 Olympic Winter Games, after which it was discontinued as an Olympic discipline. Skeleton was reintroduced at the 2002 Olympic Winter Games, with both Men' s and Women' s events, and has been held in every edition of Olympic Winter Games ever since. Skeleton is so-named as the first metal sleds introduced in 1892 were said to resemble a human skeleton.

钢架雪车在 1928 年圣莫里茨冬奥会上首次亮相，之后又出现在 1948 年冬奥会上，但此后未再作为奥运项目出现。直到 2002 年冬奥会，钢架雪车重新纳入奥运项目，设置了男子和女子小项，并出现在此后的每一届冬奥会中。钢架雪车之所以如此命名，是因为据说 1892 年推出的第一款金属雪橇类似于人类的骨骼。

The Great Britain is the only nation to have won a medal every time Skeleton events were held at the Olympic Winter Games, and has won at least one medal in each of the five competitions of Women' s Skeleton since its introduction, with five different athletes winning each medal.

英国是唯一在每一届有钢架雪车项目的冬奥会上都获得奖牌的国家，并且在女子钢架雪车入奥以来举行的五场比赛中，每一场都至少赢得了一枚奖牌，而且是由五位不同的运动员获得。

The equipment used in the Skeleton includes skeleton-specific helmet[3], which is made of fibreglass and fully covers the face, a race suit made of durable synthetic fabric with aerodynamic features, the special shoes with spikes[4] which guarantee a solid contact with the ice surface at the start, gloves and skeleton.

钢架雪车使用的装备包括：玻璃纤维制成的可覆盖整个面部的钢架雪车专用头盔、耐用的合成纤维制成的具有空气动力学特征的赛车服、能够确保出发时与冰面牢固接触的带钢钉的专用鞋、手套和钢架雪车。

IBSF restricted the materials with which skeleton sleds are permitted to be made. Sled frames must be made of steel, excluding steering or braking. The base plate, however, can be made of plastics. The handles and bumpers found along the sides of the sled help secure the athlete during a run. Some athletes opt to attach ballasts[5] if the combined weight of athlete and sled is lower than the maximum combined weight. These ballasts may only be added to the sled, instead of the rider.

国际雪车联合会对制造钢架雪车雪橇的材料作出限制。雪橇车架必须由钢制成，不包括舵或制动机构。但底板可以由塑料制成。雪橇侧面的橇鞍和橇耳有助于在比赛过程中保护运动员。如果运动员和雪橇的总重量低于最大总重量，部分运动员会选择安装压板材料。这些压板材料只能添加到雪橇上，不能放在运动员身上。

Vocabulary | 词汇

1. Skeleton [ˈskelɪtn] *n.* 钢架雪车
2. prone [prəʊn] *adj.* 俯卧
3. helmet [ˈhelmɪt] *n.* 头盔
4. spike [spaɪk] *n.* 钢钉
5. ballast [ˈbæləst] *n.* 压板材料

Language Use | 语言使用

opt to 选择

Many workers opted to leave jobs rather than take a pay cut.

许多工人宁愿离职也不接受减薪。

Lesson 15 Luge
第十五课　雪橇

Luge[1] is a discipline of the Olympic Winter Games where a competitor or a two-person crew rides a flat sled while lying supine[2] (face up) and feet first. Luge riders hurtle[3] down a slippery ice track at a high speed, relying on reflexes for steering. Unlike Bobsleigh, the Luge has no protection for potential errors made by athletes. The discipline is contested on a specially designed ice track that allows gravity to increase the sled' s speed. The winner normally completes all the runs with the fastest overall time.

雪橇是冬奥会项目，比赛时一名运动员或两人团队以双脚向前的仰卧（面朝上）姿势在平底雪橇上滑行。运动员在光滑的冰道上高速下滑，依靠反应来掌舵。与雪车不同的是，其并未对运动员可能出现的失误设置防护。这项运动在特别设计的冰道上举行，可以利用重力提升速度。滑完全程耗时最短的运动员获胜。

Athletes lie on their backs on a tiny sled with their feet stretched out in front of them, and racing down an icy track at an average speed of 140 km/h without brakes. As well as the Singles, there is a Doubles event, where the athlete with a larger build will lie on top for a better aerodynamic effect. The sport of Luge is governed by the International Luge Federation (FIL).

运动员仰面躺在一个雪橇上，双脚向前伸展，以平均 140 千米每时的速度沿着冰道向下滑行，没有刹车。比赛设有单人和双人小项，双人项目的两名队员中体型较大的一人躺在上面以获得更好的空气动力效应。雪橇运动由国际雪橇联合会（FIL）管理。

Luge is one of the oldest winter sports and has its origins in Switzerland. Luge is the French word for "sledge" and, like Bobsleigh, it was developed as a sport in Switzerland. Its roots go back to the 16th-century, but it was not until 300 years later that the first luge tracks were built by Swiss hotel owners to cater for thrill-seeking[4] tourists. The first international luge competition was held in Davos in 1883, with competitors racing along an icy 4 km road between Davos and the village of Klosters.

雪橇是最古老的冬季运动之一，起源于瑞士。"luge" 是法语词，相当于英文中的 "sledge"（雪橇）。与雪车一样，雪橇也是在瑞士发展的运动项目。雪橇的历史可以追溯到 16 世纪，但直到 300 年后，瑞士酒店业主才建造了第一条雪橇滑行道，以迎合寻求刺激的游客的需求。1883 年，第一场国际雪橇比赛在达沃斯举行，运动员们在达沃斯和克洛斯特斯村之间的一条四千米长的结冰道路上比赛。

It was not until 1955 that the first World Championship was organised, i.e. 41 years after the first European Championships. Nine years later, Luge made its debut at the 1964 Olympic Winter Games in Innsbruck, with a mixed event, a Men' s event and a Women' s event. No change has been made to this discipline since then. Since 1976, this discipline has shared the same track with Bobsleigh. The discipline was dominated by the athletes from German Democratic Republic, who won 15 of the 21 gold medals between 1964 and 1988. One of the undisputed masters of Luge is a German, Georg Hackl, who was a gold medallist for three consecutive editions of the Olympic Winter Games, in 1994 in Lillehammer, 1998 in Nagano and 2002 in Salt Lake City.

直到 1955 年，即第一届欧洲锦标赛后 41 年，才举办了第一届世界锦标赛。9 年后，在 1964 年的因斯布鲁克冬奥会上，雪橇项目首次在奥运会上亮相，当时设有男女混合、男子雪橇和女子雪橇等小项。此后，该项目一直保持不变。自 1976 年以来，这项运动一直与雪车项目共用一条赛道。来自民主德国的运动员是这项运动的绝对霸主，他们在 1964 年至 1988 年期间赢得了 21 枚金牌中的 15 枚。一位无可争议的雪橇大师，德国人乔治·哈克尔，曾在 1994 年利勒哈默尔冬奥会、1998 年长野冬奥会和 2002 年盐湖城冬奥会上连续三次获得金牌。

Men and women currently compete in Singles events and a Doubles event. Officially, the Doubles event is open to men and women, but traditionally, men have ridden together. The events competed in the PyeongChang 2018 include Men' s Singles, Women' s Singles, Doubles, and Team Relay.

目前，雪橇设有男子和女子单人比赛和双人赛。按正式规定，男女均可参加双人赛，但传统上，一般是两名男子共同驾驶雪橇。2018 年平昌冬奥会设立的小项包括男子单人、女子单人、双人和团体接力。

Vocabulary | 词汇

1. Luge [luːʒ] *n.* 雪橇
2. supine [ˈsuːpaɪn] *adj.* 仰卧的
3. hurtle [ˈhɜːtl] *v.* 猛冲，猛烈碰撞
4. thrill-seeking 寻求刺激

Language Use | 语言使用

1. in front of 在……前面

   Wayne has a large white coffee in front of him.

   韦恩面前摆着一大杯加了牛奶的咖啡。

2. cater for 迎合，提供饮食及服务

   Special bus and rail services are being laid on to cater for the crowds.

   专门的巴士和铁路交通服务正在安排以满足群众的需要。

MODULE 3

PARALYMPIC WINTER SPORTS

单元 3

冬残奥会项目

Lesson 1 Para Alpine Skiing
第一课　残奥高山滑雪

Para Alpine Skiing is practised worldwide and features six disciplines: Downhill[1], Slalom[2], Giant Slalom[3], Super-G[4], Alpine Combined[5], and team events. Athletes combine speed and agility[6] while racing down slopes at a speed of around 100 km/h.

残奥高山滑雪是一项全球性运动，包括滑降、回转、大回转、超级大回转、全能和团体项目 6 个分项。运动员以大约每小时 100 千米的速度冲下坡道，既要快，又要保持灵活。

It is for both male and female athletes with such physical impairments as spinal injury[7], cerebral palsy[8], amputation[9], other injuries and visual impairment[10].

比赛面向身患残疾的男女运动员举办，包括脊髓损伤、脑瘫、截肢、其他损伤及视力障碍运动员。

Skiers with visual impairments are guided through the course by sighted guides using signals to indicate the direction to follow. Some athletes use equipment that is adapted to their needs including single ski, sit-ski or orthopaedic aids[11].

患有视力障碍的运动员由视力正常的领滑员使用信号引导其通过赛道。有些运动员会使用适合其需要的设备，包括单滑雪板、坐式滑雪板或骨科辅助设备。

World Para Alpine Skiing[12], formerly known as IPC Alpine Skiing, acts as the International Federation for the sport and is co-ordinated by the World Para Alpine Skiing Technical Committee.

世界残奥高山滑雪联合会（原国际残奥委会高山滑雪委员会）是残奥高山滑雪项目的国际单项体育联合会，由世界残奥高山滑雪协会技术委员会负责协调。

The first Paralympic Winter Games took place in Örnsköldsvik in Sweden in 1976 and featured two Alpine disciplines–Slalom and Giant Slalom.

在 1976 年瑞典恩舍尔兹维克第一届冬残奥会上，举行了两个高山滑雪项目的比赛——回转和大回转。

Downhill was added to the Paralympic programme in 1984 in Innsbruck, Austria, and Super-G was added in 1994 at Lillehammer, Norway. Sit-skiing was introduced as a demonstration discipline at the Innsbruck 1984 Paralympics and became a medal event at the Nagano 1998 Paralympic Games.

滑降在 1984 年奥地利因斯布鲁克冬残奥会上入奥，超级大回转在 1994 年挪威利勒哈默尔冬残奥会上入奥。坐姿滑雪作为表演项目被纳入 1984 年因斯布鲁克冬残奥会，后在 1998 年长野冬残奥会上成为奖牌小项。

Five disciplines are on the Paralympic programme: Downhill, Super-G, Alpine Combined, Giant Slalom, and Slalom.

Athletes of Paralympic Winter Games are classified as follows: LW 1–9 for standing skiers, among which LW1–4 are for skiers with leg impairments, LW5–8 are for skiers with arm impairments, and LW9 for skiers with combined arm and leg impairments; LW 10–12 for sitting-skiers; and B1–3 for skiers with visual impairments.

残奥会比赛项目包含残奥高山滑雪的 5 个分项：滑降、超级大回转、全能、大回转、回转。

冬残奥会运动员分级如下：站姿运动员为 LW1–9 等级，其中 LW1–4 适用于腿部残疾运动员，LW5–8 适用于手臂残疾运动员，LW9 适用于手臂和腿部均有残疾的运动员；坐姿运动员分为 LW10–12 等级；有视力障碍的滑雪选手分为 B1–3 等级。

Vocabulary | 词汇

1.	Downhill [ˌdaʊnˈhɪl]	*n.*	滑降
2.	Slalom [ˈslɑːləm]	*n.*	回转
3.	Giant Slalom		大回转
4.	Super-G		超级大回转
5.	Alpine Combined		全能
6.	agility [əˈdʒɪləti]	*n.*	灵活性
7.	spinal injury		脊髓损伤
8.	cerebral palsy		脑瘫
9.	amputation [ˌæmpjuˈteɪʃn]	*n.*	截肢
10.	visual impairment		视力障碍
11.	orthopaedic aids		骨科辅助设备
12.	World Para Alpine Skiing		世界残奥高山滑雪联合会

Language Use | 语言使用

adapt to　　改变；改造，使……适用于

This book should be adapted to the comprehension ability of the freshmen.

应该将本书改写一下，以便适应新生的理解能力。

Lesson 2 Para Biathlon

第二课　残奥冬季两项

Para Biathlon was introduced in Innsbruck in 1988 for athletes with physical impairments, and in 1992, athletes with visual impairments also became eligible to compete.

1988 年因斯布鲁克冬奥会引入了面向肢体残疾运动员的冬季两项比赛，到了 1992 年，有视力障碍的运动员也有资格参加比赛。

The events consist of a 2.0 or 2.5 km course that athletes can ski for three or five laps in the free technique for a total race distance between 6–15 km. Between the two laps, athletes must hit the two targets located at a distance of 10m away. Each miss is penalised by an increase in the overall route time. The most important factor lies in the capability of alternating the skills of physical endurance[1] and shooting accuracy during the competition. Athletes with visual impairments are assisted by acoustic signals[2], by which they can turn and shoot based on signal intensity. The sport is governed by the World Para Nordic Skiing (WPNS) with coordination by the World Para Nordic Skiing Technical Committee[3] following the modified rules of the International Biathlon Union (IBU).

该项目的赛道长2.0千米或2.5千米，运动员可采用自由技巧，滑行三圈或五圈，竞赛总距离为 6~15 千米。在两圈滑行之间，运动员必须击中 10 米之外的两块射击靶，脱靶一次，将增加一次总路线耗时。成功的关键在于在比赛中能够自如调节身体耐力和射击精准度。患有视力障碍的运动员会得到声音信号的辅助。根据信号强度，运动员能知道什么时候进行转弯及瞄准目标射击。残奥冬季两项运动由世界残疾人北欧滑雪会联合会管理，并由世界残奥北欧滑雪联合会技术委员会根据国际冬季两项联盟（IBU）修改后的规则进行协调。

Cross-Country Skiing first appeared at the 1976 Paralympic Winter Games in Örnsköldsvik, Sweden. In 2016, the sports were renamed and rebranded from IPC Cross-Country Skiing and IPC Biathlon to Para Cross-Country Skiing and Para Biathlon. The International Federation, formerly known as IPC Nordic Skiing, has been renamed to World Para Nordic Skiing.

越野滑雪在 1976 年瑞典恩舍尔兹维克首届冬残奥会上首次亮相。2016 年，这两项运动分别由国际残奥委会越野滑雪和国际残奥委会冬季两项更名为残奥越野滑雪和残奥冬季两项。国际冬季残奥单项体育联合会由原先的国际残奥委会北欧滑雪委员会更名为世界残奥北欧滑雪联合会。

The sports equipment used for Para Biathlon includes rifles, sit-skis, skis and targets.

残奥冬季两项的比赛器材包括步枪、坐式滑雪板、滑雪板和射击靶。

Skiers in Para Cross-Country Skiing and Para Biathlon compete in several different sport classes, depending on the activity limitation their impairments cause. The classification system is specifically as follows: LW 2–9 for standing skiers; LW 10–12 for sitting skiers; and B1–3 for skiers with visual impairments.

根据自身残疾状况所造成的活动限制，残奥越野滑雪和残奥冬季两项运动员的比赛分为多个不同级别，具体为：LW2–9 适用于站姿运动员；LW10–12 适用于坐姿运动员；B1–3 适用于患有视力障碍的运动员。

Vocabulary | 词汇

1. physical endurance　身体耐力
2. acoustic signal　声音信号
3. World Para Nordic Skiing Technical Committee　世界残奥北欧滑雪联合会技术委员会

Language Use | 语言使用

1. be/become eligible to　有资格……

   He' s only 17 and therefore not eligible to vote.

   他只有 17 岁，因此没有投票选举的资格。

2. consist of　由……构成

   All substances consist of small particles which are called molecules.

   所有的物质都是由被称为分子的粒子组成的。

3. depend on　取决于；依赖；依靠

   The length of time spent exercising depends on the sport you are training for.

   运动的时长取决于你选择的体育项目。

Lesson 3 Para Cross-Country Skiing

第三课　残奥越野滑雪

Para Cross-Country Skiing is an adaptation of Cross-Country Skiing for athletes with disabilities. Para Cross-Country Skiing is one of the two Nordic skiing disciplines in the Paralympic Winter Games; the other is Para Biathlon. The competition is governed by the International Paralympic Committee (IPC).

残奥越野滑雪是对越野滑雪进行调整以适应残障运动员的体育项目，是冬残奥会北欧滑雪的两个分项之一，另一个分项是残奥冬季两项。该项目的比赛由国际残奥委会（IPC）管理。

According to the IPC, Para Cross-Country Skiing was introduced at the 1976 Paralympic Winter Games in Örnsköldsvik, Sweden, initially using the classic technique[1]. Skating was first approved at the Innsbruck 1984 Paralympic Winter Games and became a "medal race" in 1992 in Albertville, France. In the Lillehammer 1994 Paralympic Winter Games, Nordic skiers first competed in the same venue used for the associated Olympic Winter Games.

据国际残奥委会资料，残奥越野滑雪最早于 1976 年在瑞典恩舍尔兹维克举行的首届冬残奥会上亮相，当初使用的是传统技术。在 1984 年因斯布鲁克冬残奥会上，采用蹬冰技术的越野滑雪首次获得批准，并在 1992 年的法国阿尔贝维尔冬残奥会上成为"奖牌项目"。在 1994 年利勒哈默尔冬残奥会上，北欧滑雪项目的运动员首次在同年冬奥会举办该项目的场馆进行比赛。

Para Cross-Country Skiing includes standing events, sitting events (for wheelchair users), and events for visually impaired athletes under the rules of the International Paralympic Committee. These are divided into several categories for people who are missing limbs, have amputations, are blind, or have any other physical disabilities.

根据国际残奥委会的规定，残奥越野滑雪分为站姿、坐姿（轮椅运动员）和视力障碍项目，并根据运动员残疾情况进一步划分为多个类别，包括肢体缺损、截肢、失明或其他身体残疾。

Standing skiers use the two basic techniques in Cross-Country Skiing: classic technique and the free technique[2]. Sitting-skiers ride on sleds with skis designed for classic technique tracks, propelling themselves with poles. Skiers compete in Men' s and Women' s individual events over short, middle and long distances ranging from 1.1 kilometres to 20 kilometres based on the type of the event. Standing skiers compete in events of varying lengths–sprint (ca.1,200m), middle (10km, men and 5km, women) and long (20km, men and 15km, women). Sitting-skiers compete in events of shorter lengths–sprint (ca. 800m), middle (10km, men and 5km, women) and long (15km, men and 12km, women).

站姿运动员使用传统式和自由式两种越野滑雪基本技术。坐姿运动员使用的雪橇配有为传统赛道设计的滑雪板，依靠滑雪杖推动前行。比赛包括男子和女子个人短、中、长距离的不同小项，距离 1.1~20 公里不等。站姿运动员参与的小项距离各不相同——短距离约 1200 米，中距离为男子 10 公里、女子 5 公里，而长距离为男子 20 公里、女子 15 公里。坐姿运动员参与的小项距离较短，短距离约 800 米，中距离为男子 10 公里、女子 5 公里，长距离为男子 15 公里、女子 12 公里。

Sitting-skiers compete in a sitting position using a sit-ski, which has a chair supported with a suspension over a pair of skis that ride in a track; athletes are secured to the sit-ski by strappings. Standing skiers use conventional Cross-Country racing skis, which are of fibreglass-composite structure[3].

坐姿运动员坐在坐式滑雪器上比赛。坐式滑雪器是利用悬架将座椅固定在一双滑雪板上，在赛道滑行；椅子上安装有束带保护运动员。站姿运动员使用传统的玻璃纤维复合结构越野滑雪板。

Vocabulary | 词汇

1. classic technique　　传统技巧
2. free technique　　自由式技巧
3. fibreglass-composite structure　　玻璃纤维复合结构

Language Use | 语言使用

1. be governed by　　由……管理，在……管理下

   The rights of our citizens are governed by Constitution.

   我们公民的权利是由宪法规定的。

2. be divided into　　分为……种类，把……分成……

   The human brain is divided into two hemispheres.

   人类的大脑分为两个半球。

3. propel...with...　　用……推动

   The ship was propelled forward with paddles.

   这条船靠船桨来推动前行。

Lesson 4 Para Snowboard
第四课　残奥单板滑雪

Para Snowboard is practised worldwide and features three disciplines: Snowboard-Cross[1], Banked Slalom[2] and Giant Slalom. Athletes combine speed and agility while racing down courses as fast as possible.

残奥单板滑雪是一项世界性的运动，分为障碍追逐、坡面回转、大回转三个项目。运动员体现了速度与敏捷性的结合，以尽可能快的速度滑下雪道。

Competitors include male and female athletes with physical impairments such as spinal injury, cerebral palsy and amputation.

参赛者包括身体有残疾的男女运动员，如脊髓损伤、脑瘫和截肢。

Athletes compete in three categories based on their functional ability–SB-LL1 and SB-LL2 for lower-limb impaired riders and SB-UL for upper-limb impaired athletes.

运动员根据其身体机能分为三个等级，适用于下肢残疾选手的 SB–LL1 和 SB–LL2 等级，以及适用于上肢残疾选手的 SB–UL 等级。

Athletes use equipment that is adapted to their needs, including snowboard and orthopaedic aids.

单板滑雪运动员使用适合其需要的设备，包括滑雪板和骨科辅助设备。

World Para Snowboard (until 2016: IPC Snowboard) acts as the International Federation for the sport and is coordinated by the World Para Snowboard Sport Technical Committee[3].

世界残奥单板滑雪联合会（2016 年之前称为国际残奥委会单板滑雪委员会）是该运动的国际冬季残奥单项体育联合会，由世界残奥单板滑雪联合会技术委员会负责协调。

The sport made its debut at the Sochi 2014 Paralympic Winter Games with two medal events being Women' s and Men' s Cross.

残奥单板滑雪项目在 2014 年索契冬残奥会上首次亮相，两个设置奖牌的项目是女子和男子障碍追逐。

For the PyeongChang 2018, the Para Snowboard medal events were increased to 10. Apart from the two seen at Sochi 2014, 6 Men' s events and 4 Women' s events were included.

在 2018 年平昌冬残奥会上，残奥单板滑雪的奖牌小项从 2014 年索契冬奥会的两项增加到 10 项，其中男子 6 项，女子 4 项。

Impairment types currently covered within the Para Snowboard are impaired muscle power, impaired range of motion, limb deficiency, ataxia[4], leg-length difference, hypertonia[5] and athetosis[6].

目前残奥单板滑雪项目的残疾类别包括肌肉力量受损、运动范围受限、肢体缺失、共济失调、腿长差异、张力亢进及手足徐动症。

Para Snowboard currently offers three sport classes, two for athletes with leg impairments and one for athletes with arm impairments.

残奥单板滑雪分为三个级别，其中两个级别适用于腿部残疾运动员，一个级别适用于手臂残疾运动员。

Vocabulary | 词汇

1. Snowboard-Cross 障碍追逐
2. Banked Slalom 坡面回转
3. World Para Snowboard Sport Technical Committee
   世界残奥单板滑雪联合会技术委员会
4. ataxia [əˈtæksiə] *n.* 共济失调
5. hypertonia [ˌhaɪpɚˈtonɪə] *n.* 张力亢进
6. athetosis [ˌæθəˈtosɪs] *n.* 手足徐动症

Language Use | 语言使用

compete in 参与……比赛

It is important to know the physics of bowling if you want to compete in the sport.

如果你想参加保龄球比赛，了解保龄球的物理原理是很重要的。

Lesson 5 Para Ice Hockey
第五课　残奥冰球

Para Ice Hockey[1] (originally known as Sledge Hockey[2]) is an adaptation of Ice Hockey designed for players who have a physical disability. Invented in the early 1960s at a rehabilitation centre[3] in Stockholm, Sweden, Para Ice Hockey is played under similar rules to Ice Hockey. Athletes are seated on sledge and use special hockey sticks with metal "teeth" on the tips of their handles to navigate on the ice.

Two men from Sweden designed the sledge in the 1960s because they wanted to continue to play hockey despite their physical disabilities. Their design included two skate blades on a metal frame that allowed the puck to pass underneath. They completed the ensemble by including two round poles with bike handles for sticks. Although there are many restrictions to the measurements and weight of the sledge used in the Paralympic Games, the basic design of modern sledge remains true to the original 1960' s simple sleds for kids. These sleds were then used in hockey. Even though in the following years people showed little interest in and awareness of sledge hockey, Europe still managed to held a Sledge Hockey competition in 1971 and five teams took part in the event. In 1981, the U.K. established their first Sledge Hockey team, and that was shortly followed by Canada in 1982. It was not until 1990 that the United States developed their first Sledge Hockey team. As Sledge Hockey continued to expand, both Estonia and Japan set up their teams in 1993. Sledge Hockey was intro-

残奥冰球（原名冰橇冰球）是专为残疾运动员设计的冰球运动。残奥冰球由瑞典斯德哥尔摩一家康复中心在 20 世纪 60 年代初发明，比赛规则与标准冰球相似，运动员坐在冰橇上，使用手柄顶端带有金属“齿”的专用冰球杆在冰上滑行。

20 世纪 60 年代，瑞典的两位残疾人士虽然身患残疾但仍想继续打冰球，他们为此设计了冰橇，冰橇上有一双固定在金属框架上的滑冰鞋，方便冰球从下方通过，另外包括两个圆杆及自行车把手。虽然残奥会对冰橇的尺寸和重量进行了诸多限制，但现代冰橇的基本设计仍然与 20 世纪 60 年代的儿童简易冰橇相差无几。这些冰橇后来在冰球运动中得以使用。虽然在随后的几年里人们对这项运动的兴趣和关注度不高，但 1971 年欧洲举行了冰橇冰球比赛，欧洲的 5 支冰球队参加了比赛。1981 年，英国组建了第一支冰橇冰球队，随后不久，加拿大于 1982 年组建了冰橇冰球队。美国到 1990 年才建立第一支冰橇冰球队。随着冰橇冰球运动的进一步发展，爱沙尼亚和日本在 1993 年组建了各自的球队。冰橇冰球被纳入 1994 年的冬残奥会，瑞典

duced to the Paralympic Winter Games in 1994, with Sweden claiming the first gold medal. Since 2010, Sledge Hockey has been a mixed-gender event.

获得了第一枚金牌。自 2010 年以来，冰橇冰球一直是一项男女混合项目。

On 30 November, 2016, the International Paralympic Committee announced that it would henceforth refer to Sledge Hockey as Para Ice Hockey. The IPC also noted that the word “sledge” had different meanings across languages.

2016 年 11 月 30 日，国际残奥委会宣布将冰橇冰球更名为残奥冰球，同时还指出，“冰橇”一词在不同语言中有不同的含义。

Essentially all of the standard rules of Ice Hockey apply to Para Ice Hockey. The differences are those necessitated by the ice sled and the athlete. The first set of international rules was created in 1990 and drafted from Canadian rules. The only penalty[4] unique to Sledge Hockey is Teeing–the act of charging an opponent using any part of the front radius of the sled. Games are divided into three 15-minute periods, followed by overtime[5] if there is a tie[6] at the end of the regulation.

冰球的所有标准规则基本上都适用于残奥冰球，只在冰橇和运动员相关规则方面存在差异。第一套国际规则创建于 1990 年，以加拿大规则为基础。冰橇冰球特有唯一罚则是罚球，即用冰橇前半径的任何部分向对手发起冲锋。比赛分为 3 个 15 分钟的时段，常规时段结束时如果打成平手，则进行加时赛。

Vocabulary | 词汇

1.	Para Ice Hockey		残奥冰球
2.	Sledge Hockey		冰橇冰球
3.	rehabilitation centre		康复中心
4.	penalty [ˈpenəlti]	*n.*	罚球
5.	overtime [ˈəʊvətaɪm]	*n.*	加时赛
6.	tie [taɪ]	*n.*	平手，平局

Language Use | 语言使用

1. allow...to... 允许……，使……能够……

   Allow me to introduce my wife to you.

   请允许我向你们介绍我的太太。

2. remain true to... 坚持……，忠于……，依照……

   We remain true to our commitment: Whatever we promised to do, we would do it.

   我们忠于我们的承诺：凡是答应做的，我们都会做到。

Lesson 6 Wheelchair Curling
第六课　轮椅冰壶

Wheelchair Curling[1] is an adaptation of Curling for athletes with a disability affecting their lower limbs or motion. Wheelchair Curling is governed by the World Curling Federation (WCF)[2], and is one of the sports in the Paralympic Winter Games.

轮椅冰壶由冰壶项目发展而来，是适合下肢残疾或行动不便的运动员的一种冰壶运动。轮椅冰壶由世界冰壶联合会管理，是冬残奥会比赛项目之一。

Wheelchair Curling began in Europe in the late 1990s and in North America in 2002. The first World Wheelchair Curling Championship was held in Sursee[3], Switzerland in 2002, and was won by the host nation that beat Canada 7 to 6 in the final. It started as a Paralympic sport at the 2006 Paralympic Winter Games in Turin, Italy.

20 世纪 90 年代后期，轮椅冰壶在欧洲出现，2002 年传播到了北美。第一届世界轮椅冰壶锦标赛于 2002 年在瑞士苏尔塞举行，东道主在决赛中以 7∶6 的比分击败加拿大队获得冠军。2006 年，轮椅冰壶在意大利都灵冬残奥会上成为冬残奥会比赛项目。

The 2009 World Championship was held in Vancouver, British Columbia, Canada, in the same venue used for the 2010 Olympic and Paralympic Winter Games.

2009 年，轮椅冰壶世锦赛在加拿大大不列颠哥伦比亚省的温哥华举行，使用了与 2010 年冬奥会和冬残奥会相同的场馆。

National and international competitions are played under rules devised by the World Curling Federation. These rules mandate[4] that teams be of mixed genders. Each game is composed of 8 ends, and limits the thinking time for each team to 38 minutes. Eligibility is limited to the disabled using a wheelchair for daily mobility–more specifically, those who are non-ambulant[5] or can walk only very short distances.

轮椅冰壶的国际国内比赛均采用世界冰壶联合会制定的规则，其要求参赛队为男女混合，轮椅冰壶每场 8 局，每队比赛思考时间为 38 分钟。只有日常使用轮椅活动的残疾运动员才有资格参加比赛——更具体地说，只有无法行走或只能走很短距离的人才能够参加比赛。

At their semi-annual meeting in April 2010, the World Curling Federation lifted their ban on the use of power chairs at WCF sanctioned events.

Wheelchair Curling can be played by people with a wide range of disabilities. A player only needs coordination to exert a measured pushing force and a tolerance for cold. It is not an aerobic activity[6]. Without the need for sweepers[7], Wheelchair Curling is well suited to two-person formats such as stick-curling[8].

在 2010 年 4 月召开的半年度会议上，世界冰壶联合会解除了在其许可的比赛项目中禁止使用电动轮椅的禁令。

轮椅冰壶运动适合多种残疾人，选手只需要具有一定的身体协调能力来施加适度的推力，并且需具有一定的耐寒能力。这项运动不是有氧运动。因为不需要扫冰运动员，轮椅冰壶非常适合两个人对决，如推杆式冰壶。

Vocabulary | 词汇

1.	Wheelchair Curling		轮椅冰壶
2.	World Curling Federation		世界冰壶联合会
3.	Sursee		苏尔塞（瑞士城镇）
4.	mandate [ˈmændeɪt]	*n.*	（强制性）要求，规定
5.	non-ambulant	*adj.*	无法行动的
6.	aerobic activity		有氧运动
7.	sweeper [ˈswiːpər]	*n.*	扫冰运动员
8.	stick-curling		推杆式冰壶

Language Use | 语言使用

1. lift the ban on...　　取消对……的限制（禁令）

   Some restaurants hope to lift the ban on smoking.

   有些餐厅希望可以解除禁烟令。

2. be well suited to...　　适用于……，适合……

   Robots are well suited to this repetitive work.

   机器人很适合这项重复性高的工作。

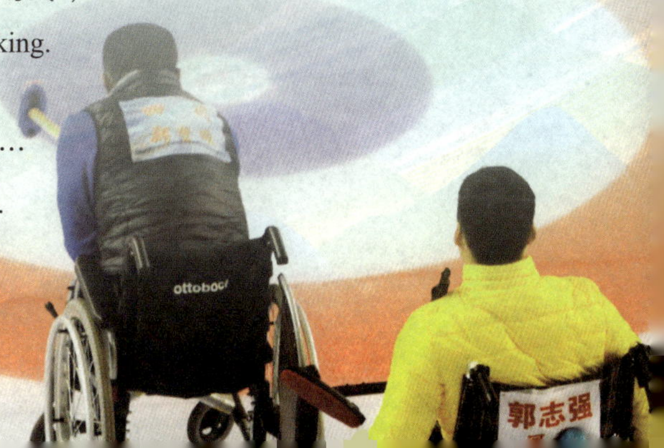

MODULE 4

200 SENTENCES OF DAILY ENGLISH

单元 4

常用英语会话 200 句

Lesson 1 Greeting
第一课　问候

First Meeting | 初次见面

1. A: Hi, my name is Charlie. It' s so nice to meet you.
   甲：你好，我叫查利。很高兴认识你。
2. B: I am Kelly. It' s a great pleasure to meet you, Charlie.
   乙：我叫凯莉。查利，很高兴认识你。
3. A: What do you do, Kelly?
   甲：你做什么工作，凯莉?
4. B: I work at the bank. How about you?
   乙：我在银行工作。你呢?
5. A: I am working for the Beijing Organising Committee for the 2022 Olympic and Paralympic Winter Games.
   甲：我为北京2022年冬奥会和冬残奥会组织委员会工作。
6. A: That' s great. We are all looking forward to watching the Games.
   乙：那太棒了！我们都盼望着看冬奥会。
7. A: But you have to wait for several months.
   甲：但你们还需要等几个月。

Meeting after a Long Time | 久别重逢

8. A: Hey Mary! It' s good to see you!
   甲：嘿，玛丽！见到你太好了！
9. B: Wow, Andy. How long has it been? Almost one year! How are you doing?
   乙：哇，安迪！多久没见了？差不多一年了吧！你还好吧?
10. A: The same as usual. How about you?
    甲：老样子。你呢?

11. B: I am quite busy at work these days, but otherwise, everything goes great.

乙：就是最近工作有点忙，但除此之外，其他都很好。

12. A: So, you finally have some free time to have fun here?

甲：那么，你终于有空来这里玩了吗?

13. B: Yeah, you know I always do some physical exercises on Saturday.

乙：是的，你知道的，我星期六一般会锻炼一下身体。

14. A: Well, have a good time.

甲：好啊，玩得开心。

15. B: You too.

乙：你也一样。

Lesson 2 Wayfinding
第二课　问路

Find the Railway Station | 寻找火车站

16. A: Excuse me, could you please tell me the way to the railway station?

    甲：请问，你能告诉我怎么去火车站吗?

17. B: Sure. But there are two railway stations nearby. One is for the high-speed trains, and the other for ordinary trains. Which one do you want to go?

    乙：好的。不过附近有两个火车站。一个是高铁站，另一个是普通火车站。你想去哪一个?

18. A: I think I should take an ordinary train.

    甲：我想我应该搭普通火车。

19. B: So, just go down this street and turn left at the third corner. The station is at the end of that street.

    乙：那就沿着这条街走，在第三个拐角处左转。走到头就是火车站。

20. A: Thank you so much for your kindness.

    甲：非常感谢你的好心帮助。

21. B: You are welcome.

    乙：不客气。

Get to a Sightseeing Spot | 去景点

22. A: Sorry to trouble you. Can you tell me how to get to the Tian’anmen Square?

    甲：很抱歉打扰你。你能告诉我怎么去天安门广场吗?

23. B: Oh, that is pretty far from here. So, I strongly suggest you take a bus.

    乙：哦，离这里很远呢。所以，我强烈建议你坐公共汽车去。

24. A: Okay, that sounds a good idea, but which line shall I take?

    甲：好的，不错的建议，那我应该坐哪路车呢?

25. B: Well, you can take the Line 1 bus from here, but then you have to walk about 10 minutes to get to the square.

乙：嗯，你可以从这里乘坐1路公共汽车，不过下车后要步行10分钟左右才能到广场。

26. A: I got it. Thanks a lot for your help.

甲：我明白了。非常感谢你的帮助。

27. B: It' s my pleasure.

乙：不客气。

Lesson 3 Dining
第三课　用餐

Be Invited to a Spanish Restaurant | 受邀去西班牙餐厅

28. A: It' s very nice of you to invite me to this beautiful restaurant.

    甲：非常感谢你请我来这家美丽的餐厅用餐。

29. B: I' m very glad you could come, Annie. Would you like to have some chicken?

    乙：我很高兴你能来，安妮。你想来点儿鸡肉吗?

30. A: Oh, thank you so much. Chicken is my favourite dish. This is the first time that I have come to a Spanish restaurant. Could you tell me how they cook chicken in Spanish style?

    甲：哦，非常感谢，我最喜欢吃鸡肉。这是我第一次来西班牙餐厅。你能告诉我西班牙风味的鸡肉是怎么做的吗?

31. B: Sure. You know in Spain people always roast chicken with special sauces.

    乙：好的。西班牙人喜欢用特殊的酱料来烤鸡肉。

32. A: That sounds great. I can' t wait to try it.

    甲：听起来不错。我要尝尝看。

33. B: Annie, would you care for another helping?

    乙：安妮，还要再来一份吗?

34. A: No more, thank you. I' m quite full.

    甲：不，谢谢。我吃饱了。

35. B: Did you enjoy the meal?

    乙：今天吃得怎么样?

36. A: It' s the most delicious dinner I' ve had for a long time.

    甲：这是我这么长时间吃过的最美味的晚餐。

37. B: I' m so glad you like it.

    乙：很高兴你喜欢。

38. A: Thank you very much for your hospitality.

甲：非常感谢您的招待。

Vanilla Cookies | 香草曲奇

39. A: John, where are the cookies? Don’ t tell me you ate them all! Again!

甲：约翰，曲奇在哪？别告诉我你又吃光了！

40. B: Yes, I did. I couldn’ t help it. They were so good.

乙：是，我吃了。我忍不住，太好吃了。

41. A: I thought you didn’ t like cookies.

甲：我以为你不喜欢曲奇。

42. B: Well, I don’ t like cookies flavoured with chocolate at all. But vanilla is different. I love them to death.

乙：嗯，我不喜欢吃巧克力味曲奇。但香草曲奇不一样。我非常喜欢香草味。

43. A: Huh, I didn’ t know that.

甲：嗯，我没觉得。

44. B: Well, tell you what, vanilla cookies taste even better with a glass of cold milk.

乙：好吧，告诉你，香草曲奇配一杯冷牛奶更好吃。

Dining out | 外出就餐

45. A: What are we going to eat for dinner?

甲：我们晚上吃什么？

46. B: I’ m going to make some pork chops.

乙：我打算做点儿猪排。

47. A: I’ m afraid the meat is rotten.

甲：我担心肉已经坏了。

48. B: That’ s strange! I just bought it the day before yesterday.

乙：不会吧！我前天刚刚买的。

49. A: Well, I forgot to put it in the refrigerator.

甲：好吧，我忘记把肉放进冰箱了。

50. B: Good for you! Now, what should we eat?

乙：你干的好事！那我们现在吃什么?

51. A: Why don’ t we eat out?

甲：要不我们出去吃?

52. B: Again? Weren’ t you just complaining that it’ s too expensive to eat out?

乙：又出去吃? 你不是才说出去吃太贵了吗?

53. A: Not when you’ re hungry.

甲：你饿的时候就不嫌贵了。

Lesson 4 Travel

第四课　旅行

Airport Check-in | 机场值机

54. A: Hello. Where are you flying to today?

甲：您好。请问您要飞往哪里?

55. B: Hi, I' m flying to Nanjing, Jiangsu Province.

乙：您好，我要去江苏省南京市。

56. A: Can I see your ticket and your passport, please?

甲：我能看看您的机票和护照吗?

57. B: Sure. Here' s my passport, and here' s my E-ticket.

乙：好的。这是我的护照和电子机票。

58. A: Thank you. Would you like a window seat?

甲：谢谢。您想要靠窗的座位吗?

59. B: No, I' d like an aisle seat please.

乙：不，我想要一个过道座位。

60. A: Okay, and is all this luggage yours?

甲：好的，这些都是您的行李吗?

61. B: These two bags are mine.

乙：这两个包是我的。

62. A: All right. One of your bags is overweight... I' m going to have to charge you for the excess weight.

甲：好的。您的一个包超重了，超重部分要另外收费。

63. B: I see. How much extra do I have to pay? Can I pay by credit card?

乙：好的。我要多付多少钱? 可以用信用卡付款吗?

64. A: 200 yuan, sir. And yes, we do accept credit cards.

甲：200元，先生。是的，可以用信用卡。

Immigration Inspection | 边检

65. A: Welcome to China. Where are you from?

甲：欢迎来到中国。您从哪来？

66. B: Germany.

乙：德国。

67. A: And what' s the purpose of your visit to China?

甲：您来中国的目的是什么？

68. B: I come to watch the Olympic Winter Games Beijing 2022.

乙：我来看北京2022年冬奥会。

69. A: How long do you plan to stay in Beijing?

甲：您打算在北京待多久？

70. B: About two weeks.

乙：大约两周。

71. A: And what do you do back home?

甲：您在本国是做什么工作的？

72. B: Pardon me? I don' t understand...

乙：抱歉，我不明白……

73. A: Your job... what do you do?

甲：您的工作……您是做什么的？

74. B: Oh, I' m a high-school teacher. I teach physics and chemistry.

乙：哦，我是高中老师，教物理和化学。

Railway Travel | 乘坐火车

75. A: Good Morning!

甲：早上好！

76. B: Good Morning! What can I do for you?

乙：早上好！您需要帮忙吗？

77. A: Can I buy a ticket to Zhangjiakou here?

甲：这里可以买去张家口的车票吗？

78. B: Sure, what time do you wish to leave?

乙：可以，您想什么时候走?

79: A: What time does the next train to Zhangjiakou leave?

甲：开往张家口的下一趟火车什么时候发车?

80. B: At 16:35, from platform 8.

乙：16:35发车，8站台上车。

81. A: Is it a direct train to Zhangjiakou?

甲：火车直达张家口吗?

82. B: No, you have to change trains at Beijing.

乙：不是，要在北京转车。

83. A: I see. One ticket to Zhangjiakou, please.

甲：好的。请给我一张去张家口的车票。

84. B: Single or return, sir?

乙：单程票还是往返票呢，先生?

85. A: One way, please.

甲：单程。

86. B: 64 yuan, please.

乙：64元。

87. A: Here you are.

甲：给您钱。

88. B: Here' s your ticket and change, sir.

乙：这是您的车票和找零，先生。

89. A: I got it. Thank you so much for your help.

甲：好的，非常感谢您的帮助。

90. B: It' s my pleasure. Have a nice trip.

乙：不客气。祝您旅途愉快。

91: A: Thanks. Bye.

甲：多谢，再见!

Hotel Check-in | 宾馆登记

92. A: Hello, my name is Dennis. I have a reservation.

    甲：您好，我叫丹尼斯，有预订的。

93. B: Yes, would you like a room facing the pool or the ocean?

    乙：好的，您是想要面向游泳池的房间还是海景房？

94. A: Is there a difference in price between the two?

    甲：两个房间价格不一样吗？

95. B: Yes, the rooms that face the ocean are 800 yuan per night, while the ones facing the pool are 600 yuan per night.

    乙：不一样，海景房每晚800元，面向泳池的房间每晚600元。

96. A: Okay, I' ll go with the one facing the ocean, please.

    甲：好的，我要一间海景房。

97. B: Three nights, correct?

    乙：您要住三晚，对吗？

98. A: Yes, that' s right.

    甲：是的，没错。

99. B: I' ll have the porter bring up your bags.

    乙：我让行李员帮您拿行李。

100. A: No, that' s fine, I' ll do it myself.

    甲：不用了，我自己拿吧。

At Reception Desk | 咨询台

101. A: I can' t open the window in my room. It seems to be stuck.

    甲：我房间里的窗户打不开了，好像卡住了。

102. B: I' ll get someone to take a look at it. Anything else?

    乙：我找人去看看。请问还有其他问题吗？

103. A: Yes, how much is the beer in the minibar? I couldn' t find a price list.

    甲：有的。迷你吧里的啤酒多少钱？我没找到价目表。

104. B: It’ s 5 yuan a bottle. Anything else?

乙：一瓶五元。还有别的问题吗？

105. A: Yes. Could you tell the people in the room next to us to be quiet at night? They were screaming all night and we couldn’ t sleep.

甲：有的。您可以让隔壁房间的客人晚上安静点儿吗？他们吵了一晚上，我们根本睡不着。

106. B: Absolutely. I’ ll ask them to keep the noise down. Anything else?

乙：当然可以。我会请他们小声一些的。请问您还有其他问题吗？

107. A: No, I think that’ s it... What time do we have to check out tomorrow?

甲：没有了，就这些……我们明天要什么时候退房？

108. B: You’ ll have to leave your room by 12:00 p.m.

乙：您必须在中午12:00之前退房。

109. A: OK. And is there somewhere we can leave our luggage until the evening?

甲：好的。有什么地方可以让我们把行李寄存到晚上吗？

110. B: Yes, you can leave them in our storage room.

乙：有的，您可以放在我们的储藏室。

Lesson 5 Weather
第五课　天气

Weather Forecast | 预测天气

111.A: Do you know what the weather is going to be like tomorrow?

甲：你知不知道明天的天气怎么样?

112. B: It' s supposed to be the same as today. I don' t think the weather will change much for the next week or so.

乙：应该和今天一样。我觉得下周的天气也不会有什么大变化。

113.A: That' s great.

甲：太好了。

114. B: Why are you so happy? Do you have anything planned?

乙：你为什么这么开心？有什么计划吗?

115.A: Yeah, I' m going to Everland with my family this weekend, so I was hoping for good weather.

甲：是的，周末我要和家人一起去爱宝乐园，所以我希望天气好。

116. B: You should know, summer is the only time of year that it doesn' t rain much.

乙：你应该知道的，一年里只有夏天不怎么下雨。

117.A: Yes. That' s why we scheduled the visit.

甲：是的。这就是我们计划出去玩的原因。

Winter-time Weather in Zhangjiakou | 张家口冬季天气

118.A: What is the average temperature in Zhangjiakou in February?

甲：张家口2月份的平均气温是多少?

119. B: It is usually about minus 10 degrees Celsius.

乙：一般在零下10摄氏度左右。

120. A: What is that in Fahrenheit?

甲：华氏温度是多少?

121. B: That would be about 14 degrees Fahrenheit.

乙：大约14华氏度。

122. A: It sounds not too bad. I' d like to stay here for my winter vacation because it' s even colder in my home city.

甲：听起来还行。我想留在这里过寒假，我家2月份的温度更低。

123. B: But the best season for Zhangjiakou is autumn, because you can see the leaves of different colours everywhere.

乙：不过张家口最好的季节是秋天，到时候你能看到到处都是各种颜色的树叶。

124. A: That sounds amazing. So, I hope I could have a longer vacation till this autumn.

甲：听起来很棒。所以，我希望我可以休假到秋天。

Lesson 6 Driving
第六课　驾车

At the Gas Station | 在加油站

125. A: What can I do for you?

甲：有什么我能帮您的吗?

126. B: Fill it up, please... Hey, how far is Chongli from here?

乙：请帮我加满油……请问，崇礼离这儿还有多远?

127. A: It' s about 100 kilometres from here.

甲：还有大概100公里。

128. B: What' s the best way to get there?

乙：去那里哪条路最好走?

129. A: Take the Yanchong Highway. That will take you all the way to Chongli.

甲：走延崇高速吧。您可以一直开到崇礼。

130. B: Thanks.

乙：谢谢。

131. A: Would you like me to clean your windshield?

甲：您需要清洗挡风玻璃吗?

132. B: Yes, please... and could you check my container as well?

乙：好的……能再帮我检查一下油箱吗?

133. A: All right... All done. That' ll be 246 yuan.

甲：没问题……都弄好了。一共是246元。

134. B: Here you go. Keep the change.

乙：给您。不用找了。

Rent a Car | 租车

135. A: Hello, ABC Car Rental. How can I help you?

甲：您好，ABC汽车租赁。有什么我能帮您的?

136. B: Hi, I want to make a reservation.

乙：您好，我想订车。

137. A: What location would you like to rent from?

甲：您想从哪里租车呢?

138. B: I am flying into Beijing Capital International Airport. Do you have a booth there?

乙：我要飞往北京首都国际机场。你们在那儿有租车点吗?

139. A: Yes, we do. What date are you flying in?

甲：是的，我们有。您哪天到呢?

140. B: I am arriving on June 22nd.

乙：6月22日。

141. A: What is your arrival time?

甲：您几点抵达?

142. B: I am scheduled to arrive at 2 p.m.

乙：预计下午2点。

143. A: How long would you like to rent the vehicle?

甲：您想租多久?

144. B: I will need it for 10 days.

乙：我需要租10天。

145. A: What size would you like?

甲：您想要多大的车?

146. B: A mid-size car, please.

乙：请给我一辆中型车。

147. A: Can I get your name?

甲：可以告诉我您的名字吗?

148. B: Yes. My name is Sang Min Lee.

乙：可以。我的名字是Sang Min Lee。

149. A: Can you spell that?

甲：可以拼写一下吗?

150. B: Last name is Lee. First name is Sang. Middle initial is M.

乙：我姓Lee，名字是Sang，中间名首字母是M。

151. A: Great. Thank you. I have reserved a mid-size car for you for June 22nd until July 1st. Is there anything else I can help you with?

甲：好的。谢谢。我已经为您预订了一辆6月22日到7月1日的中型车。还有其他可以帮您的吗?

152. B: That will be all.

乙：就这些。

153. A: Thank you for calling.

甲：谢谢您的来电。

154. B: Thank you. Bye.

乙：谢谢。再见。

Problem with Road Rage | 路怒

155. A: The woman ahead of us is driving so slowly!

甲：我们前面的那个女人开得太慢了!

156. B: People like that just drive me nuts.

乙：那种人简直能逼疯我。

157. A: Wait a minute. Do you have a problem with road rage?

甲：等一下。你是不是有路怒的毛病啊?

158. B: What about it?

乙：怎么说?

159. A: Didn' t you hear about the car accident right on this highway last week? A mother and a daughter overtook a car ahead of them, ran into an oncoming van, and got killed right away.

甲：你没听说上周这条高速路上发生的车祸吗? 妈妈带着女儿超了前面的车，结果撞上了迎面过来的面包车，当场死亡。

160. B: I did hear about that. That' s a scary story.

乙：我的确听说了。太可怕了。

161. A: So, when you drive, don' t drive like crazy. Drive with patience.

甲：所以，你开车的时候不要像个疯子一样。开车要有耐心。

162. B: Okay, thank you very much for reminding me that.

乙：好的，谢谢你提醒我。

Lesson 7 Shopping
第七课　购物

Purchase in a Boutique | 礼品店购物

163. A: Hi, are you being helped?

甲：您好，有人为您导购吗?

164. B: No, I' m not. I' m interested in some scarves.

乙：没有。我想看看围巾。

165. A: All our scarves are in this section. What do you think of this one here? It' s made of silk.

甲：我们所有的围巾都在这儿。您觉得这条怎么样? 这条是用丝绸做的。

166. B: Hm, it looks nice, but I' d like to have something warm for the winter.

乙：嗯，看起来不错，但我想看看冬天用的，暖和一些的。

167. A: Maybe you would like a heavy wool scarf. How about this one?

甲：也许您会喜欢厚羊毛围巾。这条怎么样?

168. B: I think that' s what I want. How much is it?

乙：我看这条就是我想要的。多少钱?

169. A: It' s...500 yuan.

甲：这条是……500元。

170. B: It' s a little expensive. Do you think it' s possible to get a discount?

乙：有点儿贵。您看是不是能打个折?

171. A: Hm, since you like it so much, how about a 10 percent discount? That' s the best I can offer.

甲：嗯，既然您这么喜欢，打九折怎么样? 这是我能给您的最大折扣了。

172. B: That' s good. Could you wrap it up for me?

乙：太好了。可以帮我包起来吗?

173. A: Sure. Is there anything else I can get for you?

甲：当然。还有什么我能帮您的吗?

174. B: No, that should be it. Thank you.

乙：没有了，就这些了。谢谢。

Keep the Receipt | 保留收据

175. A: Is there anything else you would like to buy?

甲：您还有什么想买的吗?

176. B: No, thank you. I guess that' s it. By the way, in case there' s a flaw in this e-book reader, can I return it?

乙：没有了，谢谢。就这了些。对了，如果我这个电子书阅读器有问题了，可以退吗?

177. A: Yes. But you must return it within 30 days.

甲：可以的。但必须在30天内退货。

178. B: Is there a charge for that? I know other stores have a restocking fee.

乙：还要收费吗?我知道别的商店会收补货费。

179. A: There will be no charge at all. However, you must show us the receipt. Could you sign it here, please?

甲：完全不收费。但是您必须向我们出示收据。您能在这里签名吗?

180. B: Thank you.

乙：谢谢。

181. A: All right. Keep your receipt. If something comes up, you can show it to us, and we' ll give you a refund.

甲：好的。请留好收据。如果出现问题，您就带着收据过来，我们会退款的。

182. B: Thanks. I' ll put it in a safe place.

乙：谢谢。我会收好它的。

Lesson 8 Hobbies
第八课　爱好

Gardening | 园艺

183. A: Hello Jack. What are you doing this morning?

甲：你好，杰克。今天早晨你打算干什么?

184. B: I am taking care of my garden. It has too many weeds.

乙：我正准备整理花园。里面的杂草太多了。

185. A: Oh! What a beautiful garden it is!

甲：哦！好美的花园啊！

186. B: Yes, it is beautiful as I work every day in it. It is my hobby.

乙：是的，因为我每天都打理，所以很漂亮。这是我的爱好。

187. A: I think it is more than a garden.

甲：我觉得这不仅仅是一个花园。

188. B: You are right. There are two parts in my garden. In one part, I have planted flowers, while in the other part I have cultivated vegetables.

乙：你说得对。我的花园有两块儿。一块儿种花，另一块儿种植了蔬菜。

189. A: That sounds great!

甲：听起来很棒！

190. B: This is very joyful. Can you tell me about your hobby?

乙：这些让我非常快乐。你能告诉我你的爱好吗?

191. A: My hobby is fishing. It improves my health, and it also makes me more patient.

甲：我的爱好是钓鱼。钓鱼可以改善我的健康，也让我更有耐心。

Collection | 收藏

192. A: Oh Mary, you are really into collecting old books!

甲：哦，玛丽，你真的在收藏旧书！

193. B: Yes, I collect rare books. It' s one of my hobbies.

乙：是，我收藏珍本。这是我的爱好之一。

194. A: It’ s a nice one! I myself am a collector too. I collect coins.

甲：很好啊！我也收藏。我收藏硬币。

195. B: Sounds fun! You must have many old coins!

乙：不错！你肯定有很多旧硬币！

196. A: Well, I’ m just an amateur. I don’ t have old coins, but I do have coins from most of the countries.

甲：嗯，我只是个业余爱好者。我没有旧硬币，但我有大多数国家的硬币。

197. B: What do you like to do in your spare time?

乙：你在业余时间喜欢做什么？

198. A: I like to watch movies. What about you?

甲：我喜欢看电影。你呢？

199. B: I listen to music. It helps me relax.

乙：我听音乐。可以帮助我放松。

200. A: Yeah, I couldn’ t agree more on that.

甲：是的，我非常同意。

MODULE 5

SCENARIO-BASED DIALOGUES

单元 5

冬奥情景对话

Lesson 1 Visa & Olympic Identity and Accreditation Card (OIAC)

第一课　签证和奥林匹克身份注册卡

A: Excuse me, in order to participate in the Olympic Winter Games in Beijing, do I need to apply for any special visas or permits?

甲：您好！我想参加在北京举办的冬奥会，我需要办理特别签证或其他证件吗？

B: To participate in the Olympic Winter Games you must be a holder of a pre-valid Olympic Identity and Accreditation[1] Card (OIAC)[2].

乙：要参加北京冬奥会，您必须要有一张待激活奥林匹克身份注册卡。

A: What functions does an OIAC serve? Will it allow me to enter China?

甲：奥林匹克身份注册卡具体有哪些功能呢？用这张卡可以入境中国吗？

B: Yes, an OIAC serves two purposes. The first is to serve as a multiple entry visa to China, throughout the duration of the Games.

乙：是的，奥林匹克身份注册卡有两个用途。首先，这张卡可以作为多次入境签证，奥运会期间凭卡可以多次入境中国。

A: What the other purpose does the card serve?

甲：还有一个用途是什么呢？

B: The second purpose of the card is to act as an identity card for the Games, which basically means it will be your principal form of identification whilst you are an athlete in the Games.

乙：第二个用途是作为冬奥会的身份注册卡，如果您是参赛运动员，这张卡就是您的身份证。

A: What if I want to enter China before the Games, or stay for an extended period after the Games have finished?

甲：假如我想在冬奥会开始前入境中国，或者我想在冬奥会结束后再待一段时间呢？

B: In this case, you must apply for your visas or residency permits by yourself.

乙：这种情况，您必须自行办理来华签证或居留许可。

A: Where can I find out more information regarding visas?

甲：我还可以通过哪些渠道了解中国签证办理信息？

B: You can refer to the website of the Ministry of Foreign Affairs of the People' s Republic of China for related provisions and visa fees.

乙：您可以访问中华人民共和国外交部的官方网站查看具体的签证政策和签证费用等信息。

A: Do I need anything other than a pre-valid OIAC?

甲：除了有待激活奥林匹克身份注册卡，还需要其他证件吗？

B: You will also need a passport that remains valid until a specific date following the conclusion of the Games.

乙：您还需要携带您的护照，并且要确保护照的有效日期在北京冬奥会结束之后。

A: Is there anything else I should be aware of?

甲：我还需要知道其他什么信息吗?

B: Before entering China using a pre-valid OIAC, you should make sure that the information on the card are consistent with what is shown on your passport.

乙：使用待激活奥林匹克身份注册卡进入中国之前，你需要确保卡片上填写的信息与您护照上的信息完全一致。

A: When will I get my pre-valid OIAC?

甲：那么，我什么时候可以拿到待激活的奥林匹克身份注册卡呢?

B: Beijing 2022[3] will distribute the cards to National Olympic Committees (NOCs)[4] that have completed their Pre-DRMs. After completion of the Delegation Registration Meetings (DRMs)[5], actual Games' participant information will be finalized by each NOC.

乙：北京冬奥组委向完成了代表团预注册会议的代表团发放奥林匹克身份注册卡。代表团注册会议结束后，各个国家和地区奥委会将确认所有参赛人员的信息。

A: If I do not participate in the Games, can I still use the pre-valid OIAC as a visa to enter China?

甲：假如我决定不来参加冬奥会了，我还能不能使用待激活奥林匹克身份注册卡作为入境中国的签证?

B: No, Beijing 2022 will cancel the information in its Accreditation System for pre-valid OIAC holders who have been confirmed not to be participating in the Games.

乙：不能，对于确认不参加冬奥会的注册卡持有人，北京冬奥组委将删除他们在注册系统里的登记信息。

A: I understand, thank you.

甲：好的，那我明白了。谢谢您。

B: You are welcome.

乙：不客气。

Vocabulary | 词汇

1. accreditation [əˌkredɪˈteɪʃn] *n.* 注册
2. Olympic Identity and Accreditation Card 奥林匹克身份注册卡，缩写为 OIAC
3. Beijing 2022 北京 2022 年冬奥会和冬残奥会组织委员会，简称为北京冬奥组委
4. National Olympic Committee 国家和地区奥委会，缩写为 NOC
5. Delegation Registration Meeting 代表团注册会议，缩写为 DRM

Language Use | 语言使用

apply for 申请；办理

Why do you apply for this position?

你为什么申请这个职位？

Lesson 2 Health Declarations
第二课　健康申报

A: What should be submitted for a team doctor for the Games?

甲：注册代表团的随队医生需要提交哪些材料？

B: A copy of valid relevant bilateral[1] agreements should be provided to the Organising Committees for the Olympic Games (OCOG) [2] as a related document when you register a team doctor.

乙：如果您注册随队医生的身份，您需要向奥运会组委会（简称为奥组委）提交一份有效的相关双方协议的副本。

A: Okay. Can my team' s doctor provide medical services to members from other teams?

甲：好的。我所在代表团的队医可以给其他代表团的成员提供医疗服务吗？

B: Yes. Team doctors can provide medical assistance and services to members of their own teams as well as members of other teams.

乙：可以，队医可以为本代表团的成员提供医疗帮助和服务，也可以为其他代表团的成员提供医疗服务。

A: What happens if a team doctor prescribes the wrong medication to an athlete or causes physical injuries through the treatments he/she provides? Will the OCOG take responsibility for this?

甲：万一队医给运动员开错了药，或者在治疗时导致运动员受伤怎么办？奥组委对此负责吗？

B: No, the OCOG will not take responsibility. Beijing 2022 will not be liable for any medical treatment administered, prescribed or performed by any team medical personnel on members of their own teams or any other teams.

乙：不，奥组委对此不负责任。北京冬奥组委不会对任何代表团医务人员为本代表团或其他代表团的成员实施的医疗管理、开的药方或进行的治疗负责。

A: But will Beijing 2022 provide medical insurance to cover malpractice[3] by team doctors?

甲：北京冬奥组委是否提供针对队医治疗不当的医疗保险？

B: Unfortunately, Beijing 2022 will not provide insurance to cover claims of

乙：很遗憾，北京冬奥组委不提供针对代表团医务人员治疗不当造成索赔的保

malpractice by team medical personnel, nor will Beijing 2022 be involved in any legal disputes that arise between any parties in this regard.

险，同时北京冬奥组委也不参与任何双方在这方面产生的法律纠纷。

A: So, who should be responsible for insurance to cover medical malpractice during the Games?

甲：那么谁承担在冬奥会期间针对治疗不当的保险责任?

B: Beijing 2022 strongly advises that all NOCs arrange adequate insurance cover for their team' s medical practitioners through their frequently used insurance agent or broker.

乙：北京冬奥组委强烈建议所有国家和地区奥委会通过自己常用的保险代理人或经纪人为本代表团的医务人员办理适当的保险。

A: Can I be sure that team doctors are qualified health professionals?

甲：我可以相信队医都是合格的医务人员吗?

B: Yes. In order to serve as a team doctor at the Games, medical personnel must be recognized as medical professionals under the laws of their respective team' s country or region.

乙：可以，要成为冬奥会的队医，医务人员必须根据所在国家或地区的法律被认可为医疗专业人员。

A: Speaking of health, do I need to make any special declarations before participating in the Games?

甲：关于健康问题，我是否需要在参加冬奥会之前办理任何特别申报?

B: No, you do not. In the event that no major epidemics occur either locally or outside of China prior to the Games, individuals arriving for the Games do not need to complete Entry-Exit Health Declaration Forms[4].

乙：如果赛前中国境内外没有爆发重大传染病疫情，参加冬奥会的个人不需要填报“出入境健康申明卡”。

A: So, what happens if a significant epidemic breaks out before the Games begin, either within China or abroad?

甲：万一在北京冬奥会开幕前中国境内外发生了重大传染病疫情，该怎么办呢?

B: In this case, the related administration department may announce a mandatory[5] inspection and quarantine requirement for people exiting or entering the country. If this occurs, you will be required to accurately fill in an Entry-Exit Health Declaration Form and undertake re-

乙：这种情况下，相关部门会发布对出入境人员实施检验检疫强制措施的公告。如果发生这种情况，您必须如实填报“出入境健康申明卡”，

quired inspections and quarantine formalities.

并接受检验检疫检查。

A: What if I am arriving from a yellow fever-affected area?

甲：假如我是来自黄热病疫区的入境人员呢？

B: In this case, you should submit a yellow fever[6] vaccination certificate that is recognised by the World Health Organisation to the Entry-Exit Inspection and Quarantine Officials upon your entry to China.

乙：这种情况下，您在入境时应该向出入境检验检疫机关出示经世界卫生组织认可的黄热病预防接种证书。

Vocabulary | 词汇

1. bilateral [ˌbaɪˈlætərəl] *adj.* 双边的
2. Organising Committees for the Olympic Games 奥运会组委会，简称为奥组委，缩写为 OCOG
3. malpractice [ˌmælˈpræktɪs] *n.* 治疗不当
4. Entry-Exit Health Declaration Form 出入境健康申明卡
5. mandatory [ˈmændətəri] *adj.* 强制的
6. yellow fever 黄热病

Language Use | 语言使用

be liable for 有……责任；有……义务

The airline' s insurer is liable for damages to the victims' families.

航空公司投保的保险公司为遇难者家庭的损失负法律责任。

Lesson 3 Olympic Village Accommodation
第三课　奥运村住宿

A: Hello, how can I help you?

甲：您好！有什么可以帮您?

B: Hi. I am an athlete that will be participating in the upcoming Olympic Winter Games Beijing 2022. I would like to know some information about the accommodation provided in the Athletes' Village throughout the Games.

乙：您好！我是一名准备参加北京冬奥会的运动员，我想了解一下冬奥会期间运动员村所提供的住宿情况。

A: Sure, what would you like to know?

甲：您想了解哪方面呢?

B: How large will the apartments for athletes in the Olympic Village be?

乙：在奥运村的运动员公寓有多大呢?

A: The apartment units will have either 3 or 4 bedrooms.

甲：每套公寓有3~4间卧室。

B: And how many bathrooms will there be in each apartment?

乙：每套公寓有几个卫生间呢?

A: According to IOC *Technical Manual on Olympic Village*, every four people have at least one bathroom. Beijing Village will live up to or exceed this standard and there will be at least one bathroom for every three wheelchair users.

甲：根据国际奥委会《奥运村技术手册》的规定，每四人至少有一间卫生间；而北京冬奥村的标准将达到或者是超过这个标准；同时，至少为每三名轮椅使用者提供一间卫生间。

B: How many people can each bedroom accomodate?

乙：每间卧室可以住几个人?

A: Bedrooms will be allotted for either single or double occupancy. Chefs de Mission will get single occupancy bedrooms.

甲：卧室分为单人间与双人间。而代表团团长将分到一个单人间。

B: Okay. Could you please also tell me how large the bedrooms will be?

乙：好的，另外，您能告诉我卧室有多大吗?

A: No problem. All single rooms will have a minimum area of 9 square metres, and double rooms will have a minimum area of 12 square metres.

甲：没问题。单人间至少有9平方米，双人间至少有12平方米。

B: I know this may sound a little odd, but I would also like to know about what type of flooring[1] is used in the apartments.

乙：这个问题听起来可能有点古怪，但是我想问一下，公寓铺的是什么地板。

A: Not odd at all. I am happy to answer all your questions. With the exception of tiled bathrooms and entrance hallway, all flooring will be covered by linoleum.

甲：这个问题一点也不古怪啊！我也非常乐意回答您所有的问题。除了卫生间和走廊铺的是瓷砖，所有地板都会铺油地毡。

B: Thank you. Also, I would like to know what furniture each apartment will be equipped with.

乙：谢谢。我还想了解一下公寓都有什么家具。

A: Sure. Each apartment will have one drying rack, and each bedroom will have one mirror. One meeting table with foldable chairs will also be provided for multi-function space in each apartment unit.

甲：没问题。每套公寓都配有一个晾衣架，每间卧室都有一面镜子。每套公寓的公共区域还会摆放一张会议桌和几把折叠椅。

B: Will there be blackout curtains installed in the bedrooms?

乙：在卧室里安装遮光窗帘了吗？

A: Yes. For the comfort and convenience of athletes, each bedroom will be installed with blackout curtains.

甲：是的，每间卧室都安装遮光窗帘，让运动员住得舒适，也方便运动员活动。

B: Great. What about keys to the apartment? Will I be provided with separate keys for my bedroom and my apartment?

乙：太好了。那么公寓的钥匙呢？会给我发卧室和公寓的钥匙吗？

A: Yes, you will. Each resident will receive a key holder with one key for their bedroom and another key for their apartment unit.

甲：会的，每位居民都会领到一把卧室钥匙和一把公寓钥匙。

B: Thanks. Also, is there a difference be-

乙：谢谢。还有，代表团团长卧室的家

tween the furniture provided in Chef de Mission bedrooms and athlete and team officials' bedrooms?

具与运动员和随队官员卧室的家具配置有什么不同吗?

A: Yes. There is slightly different furniture provided in Chef de Mission bedrooms.

甲：是的，代表团团长卧室的家具配置会有些不一样。

B: Could you please explain that to me in further detail?

乙：您能具体说一下吗?

A: Sure, no problem. Each bedroom for athletes and team officials will be furnished with one bed with mattress, one bedside table with lockable drawers[2], one bedside lamp, closet space, six clothes hangers, and a wastebasket; while Chef de Mission bedrooms also come with an office desk with lockable drawers, an office chair, a telephone, a television with an Olympic feed, a small refrigerator and an office stationery kit[3].

甲：好的，没问题。运动员和随队官员的卧室全部配有一张铺上床垫的床、一个有带锁的抽屉的床头柜、一盏床头灯、衣柜、六个衣架和一个垃圾桶；代表团团长的卧室还有一张配有带锁抽屉的办公桌、一张办公椅、一部电话机、一台可以接收奥运转播信号的电视机、一个小冰箱以及一个办公文具盒。

B: Thank you, you have been very helpful.

乙：感谢，这些信息对我很有帮助。

A: No worries, glad to to be your help.

甲：不用客气，我很高兴能够帮上忙。

Vocabulary | 词汇

1. flooring [ˈflɔːrɪŋ] 地板铺设
2. lockable drawers 带锁的抽屉
3. office stationery kit 办公文具盒

Language Use | 语言使用

with the exception of 除了……以外

With the exception of fresh agricultural products and dairy products, try not to buy any food.

除了新鲜的农产品和奶制品，不要买任何食物。

Lesson 4 Ticketing
第四课　票务

A: Hi there, I would like to ask about ticketing for the Olympic Winter Games Beijing 2022, please.

甲：您好！我想向您咨询一下北京冬奥会的售票情况。

B: Sure, you' ve come to the right place. How can I be of assistance?

乙：好啊，您真是问对人了，有什么可以帮到您？

A: Are there sales outlets available inside the Olympic Village?

甲：奥运村有售票点吗？

B: Yes. A Ticket Box Office is available in the International Zone which will provide ticketing services to NOCs throughout the Games.

乙：有的，国际区有一个售票处，可以在冬奥会期间为国家和地区奥委会提供票务服务。

A: Are sales outlets available at any other locations?

甲：其他地点也有售票点吗？

B: Yes, sales outlets are also available at competition venues, providing ticketing services to NOCs during the Games.

乙：有的，各竞赛场馆也有售票点，可以在冬奥会期间为国家和地区奥委会提供票务服务。

A: Are there any free tickets available to athletes?

甲：运动员有没有免费票？

B: Yes. A number of complimentary[1] tickets will be available to the athletes across all sports during the Games.

乙：有，冬奥会期间会向所有项目的运动员提供一些赠票。

A: Could you please tell me where I can get these tickets?

甲：能告诉我去哪里领赠票吗？

B: Of course. The NOC Services Centre in the Olympic Village will be responsible for distributing these tickets to NOCs.

乙：当然可以，奥运村的NOC服务中心专门负责将赠票发给各国家和地区奥委会。

A: What should my NOC do in order to apply for the tickets <u>on my behalf</u>?

甲：我所在的国家和地区奥委会要想替我申请免费票，应该怎么做？

B: NOCs should submit applications before 10 a.m. each day for the next day's competitions. Confirmed complimentary tickets will be available for pick-up from 5 p.m. to 7 p.m. in the afternoon.

乙：国家和地区奥委会应当在每天上午10点前申请次日比赛的赠票。经确认后，可以在当天下午5点到7点领取门票。

A: What happens to the tickets if nobody retrieves them?

甲：万一赠票没人领呢?

B: Any uncollected tickets will be made available after 7 p.m. on a first-come-first-served basis[2].

乙：无人领取的赠票会在每天下午7点后重新派发，先到先得。

A: Could you please tell me where application forms for complimentary tickets can be found?

甲：能否告诉我该在哪里获得赠票申请表?

B: Application forms will be distributed to Chefs de Mission at the DRMs. As demand for complimentary tickets is likely to be higher than the actual supply, co-operation from NOCs is essential to the efficient operation of the complimentary tickets system.

乙：赠票申请表将在代表团注册会议上发给代表团团长。鉴于需求量可能大于供应量，需要国家和地区奥委会给予配合，赠票系统才能有效运作。

A: I understand. Thank you for your assistance.

甲：明白了，感谢您的帮助。

B: You are more than welcome.

乙：乐意为您效劳。

Vocabulary | 词汇

1. complimentary [ˌkɒmplɪˈmentri] *adj.* 赠送的；称赞的
2. first-come-first-served basis 先到先得

Language Use | 语言使用

on someone's behalf (on behalf of someone) 代表某人

She gave witness on behalf of the accused person.

她替被告作证。

Lesson 5 Resident Services

第五课 居民服务

A: Welcome to the Olympic Village!

甲：欢迎来到奥运村。

B: Thank you. This is my first time to take part in Olympic Winter Games, so I am not too familiar with the services that are available to the residents.

乙：谢谢您。这是我第一次参加冬奥会，我不太熟悉这里的居民服务。

A: Well, I can give you a brief rundown of the services available if you like.

甲：如果您愿意，我可以给您简单介绍一下这里的居民服务。

B: That would be great, thank you.

乙：太好了，谢谢。

A: Firstly, there are three Resident Centres in the Village, each managed by Beijing 2022 Village Resident Centre staff.

甲：首先，奥运村里面有3处居民服务中心，都是由北京冬奥组委在中心的工作人员管理。

B: Great. When are the centres open each day?

乙：好的，居民服务中心什么时间开放?

A: One of the Resident Centres operates 24 hours a day. The other two Resident Centres will operate from 7 a.m. through to 11 p.m.

甲：一个服务中心24小时营业；另两个服务中心是早上7点到晚上11点营业。

B: Where are the Resident Centres located?

乙：这些居民服务中心在哪里?

A: I will be more than happy to show you one of the centres in a moment, but if you need to locate the centres at another time, you can refer to the Olympic Village Map for the specific locations of each Resident Centre.

甲：我很乐意稍后带您到其中一个服务中心看看；如果您想在其他时间了解这些中心的具体位置，您可以查看奥运村地图，上面会详细标注居民服务中心的具体位置。

B: Do I need to visit the Resident Centres if I require a certain service, or is there a number I can call from my apartment?

乙：假如我需要居民服务的话，我需要亲自去居民服务中心吗？或者有没有联系电话，我可以从公寓打电话？

A: Each NOC will be given a telephone number for their designated Resident Centre. Calls will be answered by the designated Resident Centre staff during operating hours. After 11 p.m., all calls will be automatically forwarded[1] to the 24-hour Resident Centre.

甲：我们会给每个国家或地区奥委会提供对应居民服务中心的联系电话，对应居民服务中心的工作人员会在服务时间内接听电话。晚上11点以后，所有的来电会自动转到24小时服务的居民服务中心。

B: OK, I understand. What kind of facilities will I find at the Resident Centre?

乙：好的，明白了。在这些居民服务中心里面有什么服务设施呢？

A: Each Resident Centre has wireless Internet access, a TV lounge, self-service laundry facilities and ice machines with plastic bags.

甲：每间居民服务中心都配备有无线上网连接、一间配电视的休息室、自助洗衣机、带塑料袋的制冰机等。

B: Great. Under what circumstances should I get in contact with my designated Resident Centre?

乙：好的，那我在什么情况下应该联系我所对应的居民服务中心？

A: You should contact the Resident Centre if you need information regarding the Olympic Village or directions to specific locations.

甲：如果您需要了解有关奥运村的信息，或者想了解村内任何设施的具体位置，您都可以联系居民服务中心。

B: What happens if I misplace the key to my assigned apartment, will the Resident Centre be able to offer me assistance?

乙：万一我找不到公寓的钥匙，居民服务中心的工作人员可以提供帮助吗？

A: Of course. That is what Resident Centres are there for. You can contact the Resident Centre for assistance if you lose or misplace your keys. You can also request key replacements from the Resident Centre. However, your NOC will be required to cover the associated costs.

甲：当然可以了，这就是居民服务中心该做的。如果您的钥匙丢了或者找不到了，您可以联系居民服务中心。您还可以向居民服务中心申请换钥匙，不过相关的费用将由您所在的国家或地区奥委会承担。

B: I know this may seem insignificant, but if I need to change used towels, will the Resident Centre be happy to take care of that?

乙：我的下一个问题可能不怎么重要，但是，假如我需要更换用过的毛巾的话，居民服务中心乐意帮忙吗？

A: Yes, that is also a service provided by the Centres. You can change used towels, request amenity replenishments[2], including toilet paper and laundry soap, etc.

甲：会的，这也是居民服务中心的服务内容之一。您可以更换用过的毛巾、申请补充生活用品，如更换厕纸、洗衣皂等。

B: Fantastic, that is good to know. Are there any other services that I should know about?

乙：太好了，很高兴知道这些。还有哪些服务我需要了解的吗？

A: Off the top of my head, there are some other services provided by the Resident Centres, including housekeeping, meeting room and medical room booking.

甲：我现在能想到的还有居民服务中心提供的其他服务，如客房服务、预定会议室和医疗室。

B: Thank you. I think I have taken too much of your time, thank you for your patience.

乙：非常感谢您！我想我已经占用了您很长的宝贵时间，感谢您的耐心解答。

A: No problem. As a volunteer, I am more than happy to help. Feel free to come to me at any time if you have any further inquiries.

甲：没关系。我是一名志愿者，我很乐意帮忙，如果您还有其他想问的，请随时找我。

Vocabulary | 词汇

1. forward [ˈfɔːwəd]	*v.*	转发，转送
2. replenishment [rɪˈplenɪʃmənt]	*n.*	补充

Language Use | 语言使用

refer to　参考；涉及；指的是

The new law does not refer to land used for farming.

新法律未提到农业用地。

Lesson 6 Doping Control
第六课　反兴奋剂

A: Hi, there. I am here to inform you that you are required to undergo sample collection for anti-doping control.

甲：您好！我是来通知您需要进行兴奋剂检测的样本采集。

B: I am willing to cooperate fully.

乙：我愿意全力配合。

A: As part of the official process, I am also required to inform you of the type of sample collection and matters that need attention before the sample collection.

甲：根据标准流程，我必须在采样前告知您采样类型以及采样过程中需要注意的事项。

B: Okay. Could you also please inform me of my rights?

乙：好的，能请您说一下我有哪些权利吗？

A: Of course. You can have a representative, and, if available, an interpreter can also be there to accompany you throughout the sample collection process.

甲：当然可以。您有权要求一位陪同人员，如果可能，还可以有一名翻译人员在场，在采样过程中全程陪同。

B: What other rights do I have as an athlete?

乙：我作为运动员还拥有其他权利吗?

A: You have the right to request a delay in reporting to the doping control station for valid reasons, like participation in a Venue or Victory Ceremony, fulfilling media commitments, competing in further competitions, completing a training session, seeking necessary medical treatment, finding a representative or interpreter, or any other reasonable circumstances.

甲：您有权申请推迟到兴奋剂检测站接受检测，前提是您有充分的理由，包括参加场馆仪式或颁奖仪式、接受媒体采访、参加后续的比赛、完成训练、接受必要的治疗、找寻陪同人员或翻译人员或其他合理的情况。

B: What happens if I do not want to comply[1]?

乙：如果我不想配合呢?

A: In that case, you will be informed of the possible consequences[2] of failure to comply.

甲：如果这样，我们会提醒您拒不配合的后果。

B: So, what are my responsibilities as an

乙：那么，作为一名运动员，我在这方

athlete in this regard? 面有什么责任?

A: You should remain under direct observation of Beijing 2022 Doping Control personnel at all times from the point of initial contact through to the completion of the sample collection procedures.

甲：从第一次接触开始到采样程序结束，您应该一直受到北京冬奥组委兴奋剂检测人员的直接监控。

B: Okay.

乙：好的。

A: You are also responsible for presenting appropriate identification, such as your OIAC.

甲：您还有责任出示适当的身份证明文件，如您的奥林匹克身份注册卡。

B: Anything else?

乙：其他还有吗?

A: You are also required to comply with sample collection procedures and report immediately for sample collection unless there is a valid reason for a delay.

甲：您还必须遵守采样程序，并在第一时间接受采样，除非您有充分的理由推迟采样。

B: Thank you for explaining that to me.

乙：谢谢您的详细解释。

A: Shall we continue with sample collection?

甲：我们可以采样了吗?

B: Yes.

乙：可以。

Vocabulary | 词汇

1. comply [kəmˈplaɪ] *v.* 服从，配合
2. consequence [ˈkɒnsɪkwəns] *n.* 后果

Language Use | 语言使用

have the right to 有权利

Do you think you have the right to talk to me like that?

你觉得你有权利跟我这样说话?

Lesson 7 Lost and Found

第七课　失物招领

A: Excuse me, I was wondering if you could help me?

甲：您好！您能够帮我吗？

B: Absolutely. How can I be of assistance?

乙：非常乐意，有什么我可以帮您？

A: I seem to have misplaced my iPad. I have searched everywhere for it, but I simply can' t find it. Do you know whether or not there is a designated place[1] where lost items are brought to?

甲：我的iPad可能丢了。我已经到处都找过了，就是找不到。您知道这里有没有专门的失物招领处？

B: Yes. All items that are found in the hotel will be delivered to the Lost and Found Office in the lobby, and will be kept and taken care of there. Do you think you lost it in the hotel?

乙：有，酒店里发现的失物都会交到大堂的失物招领处。物品会在那里储存并保管。您觉得是在酒店丢的吗？

A: To be honest, I am not sure. I could have left it behind on the bus.

甲：坦白说，我也不确定，也有可能是我丢在公共汽车上了。

B: In that case, the driver is likely to hand your iPad to the bus company. The bus drivers usually deliver the lost items found in their bus to their company.

乙：如果这样，司机很可能把您的iPad交给公交公司了。公共汽车司机通常会把车上捡到的失物交给其所在公司。

A: Is there anything I should do if I can find my iPad neither in the hotel nor from the bus company?

甲：如果在酒店和公共汽车公司都找不到，我应该怎么办？

B: Yes, you should report your lost item to the nearest police station. All lost items found by citizens are often handed to the police station nearby, and positive identification[2] will be required in order to claim back your lost item.

乙：您应该向最近的派出所报告物品丢失。市民通常会把捡到的失物交到附近派出所，领回失物时需要出示指认失物的证明。

A: Thank you for your help. I will check with these places if my iPad has been found.

甲：非常感谢。我会到这些地方问问，看看我的iPad有没有被捡到。

B: You' re welcome. I hope you find what you are looking for.

乙：不用客气，希望您能顺利找回您丢失的物品。

Vocabulary | 词汇

1. designated place 指定地点
2. identification [aɪˌdentɪfɪˈkeɪʃn] *n.* 鉴定，识别

Language Use | 语言使用

be of assistance 有用；有帮助

Susan and I are happy to be of assistance.

苏珊和我非常高兴能帮忙。

Lesson 8 Venue Access
第八课　场馆通行权限

A: Hi, there.

甲：您好！

B: Hello. Do you need any assistance?

乙：您好！您需要什么帮助吗？

A: Yes. I have a list of access codes for competition venues, but I am not sure what they stand for. Could you please explain them to me?

甲：是的，我这里有一张竞赛场馆通行权限的代码，但是我不理解这些代码代表的意义，您能为我解释一下吗？

B: Sure. I would be happy to. Which codes would you like to inquire about?

乙：当然可以。我非常高兴能向您解释。您想询问哪个代码呢？

A: Please tell me what the BLUE access code represents.

甲：请告诉我，蓝色通行代码代表什么呢？

B: No problem. The BLUE access code represents the field of play[1].

乙：没有问题。蓝色通行代码指示比赛场地竞赛区，也叫内场。

A: Okay great. Let me just jot that down. What does the RED access code represent?

甲：好的，我需要记下来。那红色通行代码代表什么呢？

B: The RED access code represents operational area.

乙：红色通行代码代表了场馆运行区。

A: Fantastic. Now, could you please tell me what the WHITE access code represents?

甲：太好了，那么你能告诉我白色通行代码代表了什么呢？

B: Sure. The WHITE access code represents general circulation area.

乙：当然了。白色通行代码代表了公共通行区。

A: Right. I' ve noticed that there are some numbers that are access codes as well. What does the access code "2" mean?

甲：好的，我还留意到这些通行代码包含一些数字。数字2代表什么呢？

B: The access code "2" represents athlete preparation area.

乙：数字"2"代表运动员准备区。

A: Okay. What about "4", "5" and "6"?

甲：好的，那数字"4""5""6"又分别代表什么呢?

B: "4" represents press area, "5" represents broadcast area, and "6" represents Olympic Family area.

乙：数字"4"代表新闻运行区，数字"5"代表电视转播区，而数字"6"代表奥运大家庭区。

A: Great. Just give me a second to note that down. Finally, what does the access code R refer to in the Olympic Village?

甲：太好了。请给我一点时间让我记下来。另外，通行代码R背后的意义又是什么呢?

B: The access code R refers to the Residential Zone.

乙：代码R指的是运动员村居住区。

A: That makes perfect sense. How will zone access privileges be assigned?

甲：那我现在全都明白了。我还想问，组委会是如何安排这些通行权限的?

B: Zone access privileges[2] will be assigned to each accredited individual in accordance with the permanent but minimum requirements for his/her role and function.

乙：组委会会根据每个注册人员在赛时要履行的职责，按照最低配置的要求来分配场馆通行权限。

A: Okay. Will any of the areas be considered restricted areas[3]?

甲：好的，那组委会将会考虑设置任何通行禁区吗?

B: Yes. Some areas will be considered and managed as restricted areas, including the field of play and doping control station.

乙：会的，有一些区域将会考虑设置成为通行禁区，并按此管理，例如比赛场地和兴奋剂检查站。

A: Great. That completes the list and answers all my questions.

甲：好的，我的问题都问完了。

B: Fantastic. Let me know if you have further questions.

乙：好的，如果您想了解更多，随时欢迎您向我提问。

Vocabulary | 词汇

1.	field of play		比赛场地
2.	privilege [ˈprɪvəlɪdʒ]	*n.*	特权
3.	restricted areas		禁区

Language Use | 语言使用

in accordance with　　依照；与……一致

The work was done in accordance with her instructions.

这项工作是依照她的指示办的。

Lesson 9 Insurance

第九课　保险

A: Hello, excuse me. I would like to inquire about what kind of insurance Beijing 2022 will provide to cover the up-coming Olympic Winter Games.

B: Certainly. I can explain that to you. Firstly, Beijing 2022 will provide free medical care for all accredited people. Meanwhile, Beijing 2022 also advises NOCs to obtain private medical insurance to cover cases that are not covered by Beijing 2022' s Olympic Family Medical Care Programme. It is suggested that NOCs consult with an insurance professional for advice on medical insurance prior to travelling to China.

A: Should non-accredited persons that are non-residents of China apply for medical insurance?

B: Yes. Beijing 2022 strongly recommends that all non-accredited persons who are non-China residents attending the Games obtain sufficient travel medical insurance coverage.

A: What about repatriation insurance?

B: Beijing 2022 will provide repatriation insurance[1] for all accredited Olympic Family members, including NOC Presidents, Secretaries General, athletes, team officials, etc.

甲：您好！我想咨询一下，为了准备即将举办的北京冬奥会，北京冬奥组委会提供哪些保险措施呢？

乙：好啊，我可以向您简单介绍一下。首先，北京冬奥组委为所有注册人员提供免费医疗服务。同时，北京冬奥组委也建议国家（地区）奥委会自行购买相关医疗保险，因为可能有些病症不在北京冬奥组委提供的奥林匹克大家庭医疗服务项目之内。在前来中国之前，国家（地区）奥委会可以咨询相关保险专业人士，并征求他们的专业意见。

甲：非注册外籍人员有必要购买保险吗？

乙：有必要，北京冬奥组委强烈建议那些来参会的非注册外籍人员自行购买旅行医疗保险。

甲：有医疗转运保险吗？

乙：北京冬奥组委为所有奥运大家庭注册成员提供医疗转运保险，包含国家（地区）奥委会主席、秘书长、运动员与随队官员等。

A: What will the repatriation insurance cover?

甲：医疗转运保险具体包括的内容是什么？

B: If the people mentioned above need to return to their home country or region for medical treatment, the insurance will cover the fees of air travel back home. Accompanying medical specialists will be provided, if required.

乙：上述人员确因救治需要返回本国（地区）时，转运保险将承担航空转运费用，必要时提供特护人员陪同。

A: What if a participating official or athlete passes away?

甲：万一出现参赛官员或运动员死亡呢？

B: If a participating official or athlete passes away, repatriation insurance will cover the costs associated with transporting the body back home. The dates of repatriation insurance coverage coincide with the Olympic Family medical care services period.

乙：万一发生死亡事件，医疗转运保险会承担将该人员遗体转运回国的费用；并且，医疗转运保险的保障期应该与奥运大家庭医疗服务保障期一致。

A: Will medical malpractice insurance[2] be provided as well?

甲：组委会还提供医疗失当保险吗？

B: All the medical staff of Beijing 2022 engaged in providing medical services at the Olympic venues and designated hospitals during the Games time will be covered by malpractice insurance.

乙：北京冬奥组委所有于赛时在奥运场馆与官方指定医院开展医疗服务的医护人员都将得到医疗失当保险的保障。

A: Does this also cover NOC healthcare staff?

甲：医疗失当保险也覆盖国家（地区）奥委会代表团医务人员吗？

B: No. Beijing 2022 assumes no responsibility for any healthcare provided to NOC team members by NOC team medical personnel. In addition, Beijing 2022 will not provide any malpractice or liability insurance[3] for NOC team medical personnel.

乙：不包括。组委会对各代表团医务人员提供给代表团成员的医疗服务不承担任何责任，且组委会不会为代表团医务人员提供任何医疗失当保险或责任保险。

A: Who will be responsible for ensuring that malpractice insurance is in place for these personnel?

甲：那么谁负责为这类人员提供医疗失当保险？

B: It is the responsibility of each NOC to ensure that malpractice insurance is in place for their healthcare staff.

乙：各国家（地区）奥委会代表团应该为代表团医务人员提供医疗失当保险。

A: Understood. Will Beijing 2022 provide liability insurance?

甲：明白了，北京冬奥组委提供责任保险吗？

B: Beijing 2022 will not provide public liability insurance for NOCs, nor will it assume any responsibility for acts or omissions by NOCs and their athletes or team officials.

乙：组委会不会为国家（地区）奥委会提供公共责任保险，也不会对国家（地区）奥委会及其运动员或随队官员的作为或不作为承担任何责任。

A: Will there be property insurance in place to protect NOCs' property?

甲：北京冬奥组委购买财产保险以保障各国家（地区）奥委会的财产安全吗？

B: Beijing 2022 will not provide insurance to cover NOCs' property and assume no responsibility for any loss or damage to NOC luggages, assets and equipment while they are in transit to the Olympic Villages or venues, in use for training or competition, and in storage at venues, hotels or Olympic Villages.

乙：北京冬奥组委不为国家（地区）奥委会提供财产保险，也不承担各奥委会和代表团成员的行李、财产和器材在下列情况中的损失或损坏：运输至场馆或运动员村；在比赛和训练使用期间；场馆、酒店或运动员村存储期间。

A: Thank you. We will follow up on this issue to make sure that all of our participants are adequately covered by insurance prior to the Games.

甲：非常感谢！我们会继续跟进这件事情，以确保我们所有的参赛人员在参赛前都购买了充足的保险。

B: You are welcome.

乙：不客气。

Vocabulary | 词汇

1. repatriation insurance 医疗转运保险
2. medical malpractice insurance 医疗失当保险
3. liability insurance 责任险

Language Use | 语言使用

coincide with 符合；与……相一致

Your desire happens to coincide with ours.

您的愿望和我们的完全一致。

Lesson 10 Epidemic Control
第十课　疫情防控

（1）

A: Welcome to our Hotel. Could you please put on your face mask and have your temperature taken?

甲：欢迎来到我们的酒店！请戴上口罩，测一下体温好吗?

B: Sure.

乙：好的。

A: Thanks for your understanding.

甲：感谢您的配合。

B: I was wondering what other preventive measures I should take for COVID-19?

乙：我想问一下，我还需要采取别的预防新冠病毒的措施吗?

A: Thank you for taking COVID-19 prevention seriously. Yes, COVID-19 prevention is of the greatest priority[1] for us. First thing, wear a face mask at all times to protect you and everyone around you. Masks help prevent the spread of COVID-19, as they catch droplets[2] exhaled[3] by an infected person.

甲：感谢您认真对待新冠疫情防控。新冠疫情防控对我们来说是重中之重。首先，最重要的是要随时戴口罩，保护您自己和您周围的人。口罩可以阻止感染者呼出的微小颗粒，帮助阻止新冠病毒的蔓延。

B: Do I need to wear it all the time?

乙：我要一直戴着吗?

A: Yes. By wearing a face mask at all times, you' ll help keep the Games safe for everyone. Of course, you can go without it when you are eating, drinking or sleeping.

甲：对。一直戴着口罩能帮助安全办赛。当然，吃饭、喝水和睡觉时可以不戴。

B: Can I socialise with my friends in the lobby?

乙：我可以和朋友们在大堂聚会吗?

A: We' d suggest not. Social distancing is very important. COVID-19 is transmitted through infected droplets in our

甲：我们建议别聚会。保持隔离很重要。新冠病毒通过人与人之间密切接触传播，咳嗽、打喷嚏、说话、

breath exhaled by coughing,sneezing, talking, shouting or singing–and is passed from person to person when we are in close contact.

B: You mean I have to minimise social interaction? That means I cannot shake hands or high-five with my friends.

A: Right. Also we would suggest that you avoid certain place. The risks of catching COVID-19 grow in crowded, poorly-aired spaces and when we spend time in proximity[4] to those who are infected with COVID-19 .

B: What if I have to be in such places?

A: If so, we would suggest wearing the mask all the time and not touching any surfaces.

B: Don' t touch any surfaces?

A: Yes. COVID-19 can live on everyday surfaces through droplets exhaled by an infected person. If we touch those objects with our hands and then touch our eyes, nose or mouth, we <u>run the risk of</u> being infected.

B: Noted with great thanks.

A: My pleasure. In fact, COVID-19 is preventable as long as we keep in mind the basics of good hygiene—regularly and thoroughly[5] cleaning our hands, disinfecting surfaces, avoiding touching our face, and covering our mouths when we sneeze or cough and wearing a face mask at all times.

B: Thanks.

A: Good luck.

大喊或唱歌时呼出的飞沫会携带并传播病毒。

乙：您的意思是我尽可能减少社交活动吗？这意味着我不能和朋友们握手或击掌了。

甲：是的。同时我们也建议您避免去一些地方。当我们身处人员密集、空气流通较差的空间或与携带新冠病毒的人近距离接触时，感染风险就会增加。

乙：要是我必须得去这些地方呢?

甲：那我们建议您一直戴着口罩，不要触摸物体表面。

乙：不要触摸物体表面?

甲：是的。新冠病毒可以通过感染者呼出的飞沫在物体表面存活。如果我们用手触碰了这些物体，再去接触眼部和口鼻时，就可能被感染。

乙：了解了，多谢!

甲：不客气。其实，新冠病毒完全可以预防，只要我们牢记保持良好卫生的基本原则——勤洗手、定期消毒、避免触摸面部、打喷嚏或咳嗽时捂住口鼻，并一直戴口罩。

乙：谢谢。

甲：祝您好运。

（2）

A: Hi, I am calling to ask about the COVID-19 protocols[6] for the press.

甲：您好，我想了解一下新闻人员的新冠疫情防控规范。

B: Hello, thanks for calling. There are a number of protocols to follow before you arrive, when you arrive, while you work here and when you leave.

乙：感谢您的来电。无论是您入境前、入境时、工作时和离开时都有一些规范。

A: OK. May I know the details?

甲：好的，可以告知我细节吗?

B: Sure. Have you contacted your COVID-19 liaison[7] officer? For every accredited press, a COVID-19 liaison officer has already been appointed. This officer is trained to walk you through all the necessary processes.

乙：没问题。您联系过您的新冠防控联络官吗? 每个注册媒体都指定了一名新冠防控联络官，可以帮您完成各种必要的程序。

A: OK. I will contact the officer later, but I was wondering if I need to get vaccinated[8]?

甲：好的，我稍后会联系。我想问一下我需要接种疫苗吗?

B: We would suggest getting vaccinated before your travel. Vaccination helps protect you and the people in contact with you. Also if you are fully vaccinated, you may not need to undergo a long quarantine[9].

乙：我们建议您出发前接种疫苗。接种疫苗帮助保护您和与您接触的人。同时，如果您已经完成疫苗接种，您可能不需要接受长时间的隔离。

A: Does that mean I can move about when I arrive?

甲：那是不是抵达后我就可以随便走动了?

B: I am afraid not. Vaccination can protect you from severe symptoms, but you can still be infected but asymptomatic[10], or showing no symptoms. So you will have to stay in a bubble[11], and can only travel from bubble to bubble.

乙：恐怕还不行，接种疫苗可以保护您不得重症，但您可能会无症状感染，或者说不显示任何症状。您还得待在闭环之内，并且在闭环之内行动。

A: OK. I get it. Anything else I need to know?

甲：明白了，还有别的我需要了解的吗?

B: Well, maybe you may wish to contact your liaison officer or consult the playbook.

乙：嗯，您可以联络新冠防控联络官或者参考《疫情防控规则手册》。

A: Where can I find the playbook?

甲：我在哪儿可以找到规则手册?

B: In the official website, and you can also find other related information.

乙：在官方网站上可以找到，您也可以找到其他相关信息。

A: Thank you for all the information. I will check the website for details

甲：非常感谢您提供的信息，我会到网站上查找详细信息。

B: Good luck.

乙：祝您好运。

Vocabulary | 词汇

1.priority [praɪˈɒrəti]	*n.*	优先事项；最重要的事
2.droplet [ˈdrɒplət]	*n.*	小滴
3.exhale [eksˈheɪl]	*v.*	呼出，吐出 (肺中的空气、烟等)；呼气
4.proximity [prɒkˈsɪməti]	*n.*	(时间或空间) 接近，邻近，靠近
5.thoroughly [ˈθʌrəli]	*adv.*	彻底；完全
6.protocol [ˈprəʊtəkɒl]	*n.*	规程，规约
7.liaison [liˈeɪzn]	*n.*	联络；联系；联络员；联系人
8.vaccinate [ˈvæksɪneɪt]	*v.*	给……接种疫苗
vaccine [ˈvæksiːn]	*n.*	疫苗
fully vaccinated		完成疫苗接种
9.quarantine [ˈkwɒrəntiːn]	*n.*	(为防传染的) 隔离期；检疫
10.asymptomatic [ˌeɪsɪmptəˈmætɪk]	*adj.*	无症状的
11.bubble [ˈbʌbl]	*n.*	气泡；（引申）封闭圈

Language Use | 语言使用

run the risk of　　冒……的风险

We don’t want to run the risk of losing their business.

我们不想冒险失去他们的生意。

APPENDIX

附录

Appendix: Terminology
附录：术语

Beijing 2022 Olympic Winter Games Event	北京 2022 冬奥会项目
Alpine Skiing	高山滑雪
Alpine Skiing Men’ s Downhill	高山滑雪男子滑降
Alpine Skiing Women’ s Downhill	高山滑雪女子滑降
Alpine Skiing Men’ s Super-G	高山滑雪男子超级大回转
Alpine Skiing Women’ s Super-G	高山滑雪女子超级大回转
Alpine Skiing Men’ s Giant Slalom	高山滑雪男子大回转
Alpine Skiing Women’ s Giant Slalom	高山滑雪女子大回转
Alpine Skiing Men’ s Slalom	高山滑雪男子回转
Alpine Skiing Women’ s Slalom	高山滑雪女子回转
Alpine Skiing Men’ s Alpine Combined	高山滑雪男子全能
Alpine Skiing Women’ s Alpine Combined	高山滑雪女子全能
Alpine Skiing Mixed Team Parallel	高山滑雪混合团体
Freestyle Skiing	自由式滑雪
Freestyle Men’ s Aerials	自由式滑雪男子空中技巧
Freestyle Women’ s Aerials	自由式滑雪女子空中技巧
Freestyle Mixed Team Aerials	自由式滑雪空中技巧混合团体
Freestyle Men’ s Moguls	自由式滑雪男子雪上技巧
Freestyle Women’ s Moguls	自由式滑雪女子雪上技巧
Freestyle Men’ s Ski Cross	自由式滑雪男子障碍追逐
Freestyle Women’ s Ski Cross	自由式滑雪女子障碍追逐
Freeski Men’ s Halfpipe	自由式滑雪男子 U 型场地技巧
Freeski Women’ s Halfpipe	自由式滑雪女子 U 型场地技巧
Freeski Men’ s Slopestyle	自由式滑雪男子坡面障碍技巧
Freeski Women’ s Slopestyle	自由式滑雪女子坡面障碍技巧
Freeski Men’ s Big Air	自由式滑雪男子大跳台
Freeski Women’ s Big Air	自由式滑雪女子大跳台
Snowboard	单板滑雪
Snowboard Men’ s Parallel Giant Slalom	单板滑雪男子平行大回转
Snowboard Women’ s Parallel Giant Slalom	单板滑雪女子平行大回转
Men’ s Snowboard Cross	单板滑雪男子障碍追逐
Women’ s Snowboard Cross	单板滑雪女子障碍追逐
Snowboard Cross Mixed Team	单板滑雪障碍追逐混合团体
Snowboard Men’ s Halfpipe	单板滑雪男子 U 型场地技巧
Snowboard Women’ s Halfpipe	单板滑雪女子 U 型场地技巧
Snowboard Men’ s Slopestyle	单板滑雪男子坡面障碍技巧

Snowboard Women’s Slopestyle	单板滑雪女子坡面障碍技巧
Snowboard Men’s Big Air	单板滑雪男子大跳台
Snowboard Women’s Big Air	单板滑雪女子大跳台
Ski Jumping	跳台滑雪
Ski Jumping Men’s Normal Hill Individual	跳台滑雪男子个人标准台
Ski Jumping Women’s Normal Hill Individual	跳台滑雪女子个人标准台
Ski Jumping Men’s Large Hill Individual	跳台滑雪男子个人大跳台
Ski Jumping Men’s Team	跳台滑雪男子团体
Ski Jumping Mixed Team	跳台滑雪混合团体
Cross-Country Skiing	越野滑雪
Cross-Country Skiing Men’s 15 km + 15 km Skiathlon	越野滑雪男子双追逐（15 公里传统技术 +15 公里自由技术）
Cross-Country Skiing Women’s 7.5 km + 7.5 km Skiathlon	越野滑雪女子双追逐（7.5 公里传统技术 +7.5 公里自由技术）
Cross-Country Skiing Men’s Sprint Free	越野滑雪男子个人短距离(自由技术）
Cross-Country Skiing Women’s Sprint Free	越野滑雪女子个人短距离(自由技术）
Cross-Country Skiing Men’s Team Sprint Classic	越野滑雪男子团体短距离(传统技术）
Cross-Country Skiing Women’s Team Sprint Classic	越野滑雪女子团体短距离(传统技术）
Cross-Country Skiing Men’s 4×10 km Relay	越野滑雪男子 4 × 10 公里接力
Cross-Country Skiing Women’s 4×5 km Relay	越野滑雪女子 4 × 5 公里接力
Cross-Country Skiing Men’s 15 km Classic	越野滑雪男子 15 公里（传统技术）
Cross-Country Skiing Women’s 10 km Classic	越野滑雪女子 10 公里（传统技术）
Cross-Country Skiing Men’s 50 km Mass Start Free	越野滑雪男子 50 公里集体出发（自由技术）
Cross-Country Skiing Women’s 30 km Mass Start Free	越野滑雪女子 30 公里集体出发（自由技术）
Nordic Combined	北欧两项
Nordic Combined Individual Gundersen Normal Hill / 10 km	北欧两项个人 - 跳台滑雪标准台 / 越野滑雪 10 公里
Nordic Combined Individual Gundersen Large Hill / 10 km	北欧两项个人 - 跳台滑雪大跳台 / 越野滑雪 10 公里
Nordic Combined Team Gundersen Large Hill / 4×5 km	北欧两项团体 - 跳台滑雪大跳台 / 越野滑雪 4 × 5 公里接力
Short Track Speed Skating	短道速滑
Short Track Speed Skating Men’s 500 m	短道速滑男子 500 米
Short Track Speed Skating Women’s 500 m	短道速滑女子 500 米
Short Track Speed Skating Men’s 1000 m	短道速滑男子 1000 米
Short Track Speed Skating Women’s 1000 m	短道速滑女子 1000 米
Short Track Speed Skating Men’s 1500 m	短道速滑男子 1500 米
Short Track Speed Skating Women’s 1500 m	短道速滑女子 1500 米

Short Track Speed Skating Men's 5000 m Relay	短道速滑男子 5000 米接力
Short Track Speed Skating Women's 3000 m Relay	短道速滑女子 3000 米接力
Short Track Speed Skating Mixed Team Relay	短道速滑混合团体接力
Speed Skating	速度滑冰
Speed Skating Men's 500 m	速度滑冰男子 500 米
Speed Skating Women's 500 m	速度滑冰女子 500 米
Speed Skating Men's 1000 m	速度滑冰男子 1000 米
Speed Skating Women's 1000 m	速度滑冰女子 1000 米
Speed Skating Men's 1500 m	速度滑冰男子 1500 米
Speed Skating Women's 1500 m	速度滑冰女子 1500 米
Speed Skating Men's 5000 m	速度滑冰男子 5000 米
Speed Skating Women's 3000 m	速度滑冰女子 3000 米
Speed Skating Men's 10000 m	速度滑冰男子 10000 米
Speed Skating Women's 5000 m	速度滑冰女子 5000 米
Speed Skating Men's Team Pursuit	速度滑冰男子团体追逐
Speed Skating Women's Team Pursuit	速度滑冰女子团体追逐
Speed Skating Men's Mass Start	速度滑冰男子集体出发
Speed Skating Women's Mass Start	速度滑冰女子集体出发
Figure Skating	花样滑冰
Figure Skating Men's Single Skating	花样滑冰男子单人滑
Figure Skating Women's Single Skating	花样滑冰女子单人滑
Figure Skating Pair Skating	花样滑冰双人滑
Figure Skating Ice Dance	花样滑冰冰上舞蹈
Figure Skating Team Event	花样滑冰团体赛
Ice Hockey	冰球
Ice Hockey Men's Tournament	男子冰球
Ice Hockey Women's Tournament	女子冰球
Curling	冰壶
Men's Curling	男子冰壶
Women's Curling	女子冰壶
Mixed Doubles Curling	混合双人冰壶
Bobsleigh	雪车
2-Man Bobsleigh	男子双人雪车
4-Man Bobsleigh	四人雪车
Women's Monobob	女子单人雪车
2-Woman Bobsleigh	女子双人雪车
Skeleton	钢架雪车
Men's Skeleton	男子钢架雪车

Women' s Skeleton	女子钢架雪车
Luge	雪橇
Luge Men' s Singles	男子单人雪橇
Luge Women' s Singles	女子单人雪橇
Luge Doubles	双人雪橇
Luge Team Relay	雪橇团体接力
Biathlon	冬季两项
Biathlon Men' s 10 km Sprint	冬季两项男子 10 公里短距离
Biathlon Women' s 7.5 km Sprint	冬季两项女子 7.5 公里短距离
Biathlon Men' s 20 km Individual	冬季两项男子 20 公里个人
Biathlon Women' s 15 km Individual	冬季两项女子 15 公里个人
Biathlon Men' s 12.5 km Pursuit	冬季两项男子 12.5 公里追逐
Biathlon Women' s 10 km Pursuit	冬季两项女子 10 公里追逐
Biathlon Men' s 15 km Mass Start	冬季两项男子 15 公里集体出发
Biathlon Women' s 12.5 km Mass Start	冬季两项女子 12.5 公里集体出发
Biathlon Men' s 4×7.5 km Relay	冬季两项男子 4 × 7.5 公里接力
Biathlon Women' s 4×6 km Relay	冬季两项女子 4 × 6 公里接力
Biathlon 2×6 km W+2×7.5 km M Mixed Relay	冬季两项混合接力（女子 2 × 6 公里 + 男子 2 × 7.5 公里）
Beijing 2022 Paralymic Winter Games Event	北京 2022 冬残奥会项目
Para Alpine Skiing	残奥高山滑雪
Para Alpine Skiing Men' s Downhill, Standing	残奥高山滑雪男子滑降—站姿
Para Alpine Skiing Men' s Downhill, Sitting	残奥高山滑雪男子滑降—坐姿
Para Alpine Skiing Men' s Downhill, Visually Impaired	残奥高山滑雪男子滑降—视障
Para Alpine Skiing Men' s Super-G, Standing	残奥高山滑雪男子超级大回转—站姿
Para Alpine Skiing Men' s Super-G, Sitting	残奥高山滑雪男子超级大回转—坐姿
Para Alpine Skiing Men' s Super-G, Visually Impaired	残奥高山滑雪男子超级大回转—视障
Para Alpine Skiing Men' s Giant Slalom, Standing	残奥高山滑雪男子大回转—站姿
Para Alpine Skiing Men' s Giant Slalom, Sitting	残奥高山滑雪男子大回转—坐姿
Para Alpine Skiing Men' s Giant Slalom, Visually Impaired	残奥高山滑雪男子大回转—视障
Para Alpine Skiing Men' s Slalom, Standing	残奥高山滑雪男子回转—站姿
Para Alpine Skiing Men' s Slalom, Sitting	残奥高山滑雪男子回转—坐姿
Para Alpine Skiing Men' s Slalom, Visually Impaired	残奥高山滑雪男子回转—视障
Para Alpine Skiing Men' s Super Combined, Standing	残奥高山滑雪男子全能—站姿
Para Alpine Skiing Men' s Super Combined, Sitting	残奥高山滑雪男子全能—坐姿
Para Alpine Skiing Men' s Super Combined, Visually Impaired	残奥高山滑雪男子全能—视障
Para Alpine Skiing Women' s Downhill, Standing	残奥高山滑雪女子滑降—站姿
Para Alpine Skiing Women' s Downhill, Sitting	残奥高山滑雪女子滑降—坐姿

Para Alpine Skiing Women' s Downhill, Visually Impaired	残奥高山滑雪女子滑降—视障
Para Alpine Skiing Women' s Super-G, Standing	残奥高山滑雪女子超级大回转—站姿
Para Alpine Skiing Women' s Super-G, Sitting	残奥高山滑雪女子超级大回转—坐姿
Para Alpine Skiing Women' s Super-G, Visually Impaired	残奥高山滑雪女子超级大回转—视障
Para Alpine Skiing Women' s Giant Slalom, Standing	残奥高山滑雪女子大回转—站姿
Para Alpine Skiing Women' s Giant Slalom, Sitting	残奥高山滑雪女子大回转—坐姿
Para Alpine Skiing Women' s Giant Slalom, Visually Impaired	残奥高山滑雪女子大回转—视障
Para Alpine Skiing Women' s Slalom, Standing	残奥高山滑雪女子回转—站姿
Para Alpine Skiing Women' s Slalom, Sitting	残奥高山滑雪女子回转—坐姿
Para Alpine Skiing Women' s Slalom, Visually Impaired	残奥高山滑雪女子回转—视障
Para Alpine Skiing Women' s Super Combined, Standing	残奥高山滑雪女子全能—站姿
Para Alpine Skiing Women' s Super Combined, Sitting	残奥高山滑雪女子全能—坐姿
Para Alpine Skiing Women' s Super Combined, Visually Impaired	残奥高山滑雪女子全能—视障
Para Biathlon	残奥冬季两项
Para Biathlon Men' s 15 km, Standing	残奥冬季两项男子 15 公里—站姿
Para Biathlon Men' s 15 km, Sitting	残奥冬季两项男子 15 公里—坐姿
Para Biathlon Men' s 15 km, Visually Impaired	残奥冬季两项男子 15 公里—视障
Para Biathlon Men' s 12.5 km, Standing	残奥冬季两项男子 12.5 公里—站姿
Para Biathlon Men' s 12.5 km, Sitting	残奥冬季两项男子 12.5 公里—坐姿
Para Biathlon Men' s 12.5 km, Visually Impaired	残奥冬季两项男子 12.5 公里—视障
Para Biathlon Men' s 7.5 km, Standing	残奥冬季两项男子 7.5 公里—站姿
Para Biathlon Men' s 7.5 km, Sitting	残奥冬季两项男子 7.5 公里—坐姿
Para Biathlon Men' s 7.5 km, Visually Impaired	残奥冬季两项男子 7.5 公里—视障
Para Biathlon Women' s 12.5 km, Standing	残奥冬季两项女子 12.5 公里—站姿
Para Biathlon Women' s 12.5 km, Sitting	残奥冬季两项女子 12.5 公里—坐姿
Para Biathlon Women' s 12.5 km, Visually Impaired	残奥冬季两项女子 12.5 公里—视障
Para Biathlon Women' s 10 km, Standing	残奥冬季两项女子 10 公里—站姿
Para Biathlon Women' s 10 km, Sitting	残奥冬季两项女子 10 公里—坐姿
Para Biathlon Women' s 10 km, Visually Impaired	残奥冬季两项女子 10 公里—视障
Para Biathlon Women' s 6 km, Standing	残奥冬季两项女子 6 公里—站姿
Para Biathlon Women' s 6 km, Sitting	残奥冬季两项女子 6 公里—坐姿
Para Biathlon Women' s 6 km, Visually Impaired	残奥冬季两项女子 6 公里—视障
Para Cross-Country Skiing	残奥越野滑雪
Para Cross-Country Skiing Men' s 20 km Classic, Standing	残奥越野滑雪男子 20 公里（传统技术）—站姿
Para Cross-Country Skiing Men' s 15 km, Sitting	残奥越野滑雪男子 15 公里—坐姿

Para Cross-Country Skiing Men' s 20 km Classic, Visually Impaired	残奥越野滑雪男子 20 公里（传统技术）—视障
Para Gross-Country Skiing Men' s 10 km Free, Standing	残奥越野滑雪男子 10 公里（自由技术）—站姿
Para Cross-Country Skiing Men' s 7.5 km, Sitting	残奥越野滑雪男子 7.5 公里—坐姿
Para Cross-Country Skiing Men' s 10 km Free, Visually Impaired	残奥越野滑雪男子 10 公里（自由技术）—视障
Para Cross-Country Skiing Men' s 1.5 km Sprint Free, Standing	残奥越野滑雪男子 1.5 公里短距离（自由技术）—站姿
Para Cross-Country Skiing Men' s 1.1 km Sprint, Sitting	残奥越野滑雪男子 1. 1 公里短距离—坐姿
Para Cross-Country Skiing Men' s 1.5 km Sprint Free, Visually Impaired	残奥越野滑雪男子 1.5 公里短距离（自由技术）—视障
Para Gross-Country Skiing Women' s 15 km Classic, Standing	残奥越野滑雪女子 15 公里（传统技术）—站姿
Para Cross-Country Skiing Women' s 12 km, Sitting	残奥越野滑雪女子 12 公里—坐姿
Para Cross-Country Skiing Women' s 15 km Classic, Visually Impaired	残奥越野滑雪女子 15 公里（传统技术）—视障
Para Cross-Country Skiing Women' s 7.5 km Free, Standing	残奥越野滑雪女子 7. 5 公里（自由技术）—站姿
Para Cross-Country Skiing Women' s 5 km, Sitting	残奥越野滑雪女子 5 公里—坐姿
Para Gross-Country Skiing Women' s 7.5 km Free, Visually Impaired	残奥越野滑雪女子 7. 5 公里（自由技术）—视障
Para Gross-Country Skiing Women' s 1.5 km Sprint Free, Standing	残奥越野滑雪女子 1.5 公里短距离（自由技术）—站姿
Para Gross-Country Skiing Women' s 1.1 km Sprint, Sitting	残奥越野滑雪女子 1. 1 公里短距离—坐姿
Para Cross-Country Skiing Women' s 1.5 km Sprint Free, Visually Impaired	残奥越野滑雪女子 1.5 公里短距离（自由技术）—视障
Para Cross-Country Skiing Mixed Relay 4 × 2.5 km	残奥越野滑雪混合级接力 4×2.5 公里
Para Cross-Country Skiing Open Relay 4 ×2.5 km	残奥越野滑雪公开级接力 4×2.5 公里
Para Snowboard	残奥单板滑雪
Para Snowboard Men' s Banked Slalom UL	残奥单板滑雪男子坡面回转—UL 级
Para Snowboard Men' s Banked Slalom LL1	残奥单板滑雪男子坡面回转—LL1 级
Para Snowboard Men' s Banked Slalom LL2	残奥单板滑雪男子坡面回转—LL2 级
Para Snowboard Men' s Cross UL	残奥单板滑雪男子障碍追逐—UL 级
Para Snowboard Men' s Cross LL1	残奥单板滑雪男子障碍追逐—LL1 级
Para Snowboard Men' s Cross LL2	残奥单板滑雪男子障碍追逐—LL2 级
Para Snowboard Women' s Banked Slalom LL2	残奥单板滑雪女子坡面回转—LL2 级
Para Snowboard Women' s Cross LL2	残奥单板滑雪女子障碍追逐—LL2 级

Para Ice Hockey	残奥冰球
Para Ice Hockey Mixed Team Tournament	残奥冰球混合团体
Wheelchair Curling	轮椅冰壶
Wheelchair Curling Mixed Team Tournament	轮椅冰壶混合团体
Zone	赛区名称
Beijing Zone	北京赛区
Yanqing Zone	延庆赛区
Zhangjiakou Zone	张家口赛区
Competition Venue	竞赛场馆
National Aquatics Centre	国家游泳中心
National Indoor Stadium	国家体育馆
Wukesong Sports Centre	五棵松体育中心
Capital Indoor Stadium	首都体育馆
National Speed Skating Oval	国家速滑馆
Big Air Shougang	首钢滑雪大跳台
National Alpine Skiing Centre	国家高山滑雪中心
National Alpine Skiing Centre Speed Course	国家高山滑雪中心竞速场地
National Alpine Skiing Centre Technical Course	国家高山滑雪中心竞技场地
National Sliding Centre	国家雪车雪橇中心
Genting Snow Park	云顶滑雪公园
Genting Snow Park Parallel & Cross	云顶滑雪公园回转追逐场地
Genting Snow Park Halfpipe & Slopestyle	云顶滑雪公园 U 型障碍场地
Genting Snow Park Aerials & Moguls	云顶滑雪公园技巧场地
National Biathlon Centre	国家冬季两项中心
National Ski Jumping Centre	国家跳台滑雪中心
National Cross-Country Skiing Centre	国家越野滑雪中心
Non-Competition Venues	非竞赛场馆
Beijing Olympic Village	北京冬奥村
China National Convention Centre	国家会议中心
National Stadium	国家体育场
Beijing Medals Plaza	北京颁奖广场
CTS Figure Skating Training Hall	首体花样滑冰训练馆
CTS Short Track Speed Skating Training Hall	首体短道速滑训练馆
Yanqing Olympic Village	延庆冬奥村
Yanqing Medals Plaza	延庆颁奖广场
Zhangjiakou Olympic Village	张家口冬奥村
Zhangjiakou Mountain Press Centre	张家口山地新闻中心
Zhangjiakou Mountain Broadcast Centre	张家口山地转播中心

Zhangjiakou Medals Plaza	张家口颁奖广场
OCOG Departments	**组委会部门**
Department of General Administration	秘书行政部
General Planning Department	总体策划部
International Relations Department	对外联络部
Sports Department	体育部
Media and Communications Department	新闻宣传部
Venue Planning and Construction Department	规划建设部
Marketing Department	市场开发部
Human Resources Department	人力资源部
Supervision and Auditing Department	监察审计部
Finance Department	财务部
Technology Department	技术部
Legal Affairs Department	法律事务部
Games Services Department	运动会服务部
Culture and Ceremonies Department	文化活动部
Logistics Department	物流部
Paralympic Games Integration Department	残奥会部
Media Operations Department	媒体运行部
Venue Management Department	场馆管理部
Security Department	安保部
Transport Department	交通部
Department of Opening and Closing Ceremonies	开闭幕式工作部
Village Planning and Operation Department	奥运村部
Volunteer Department	志愿者部
Accreditation Center	注册中心
Ticketing Center	票务中心
Yanqing Operation Centre	延庆运行中心
Zhangjiakou Operation Centre	张家口运行中心
OCOG Functional Areas	**组委会业务领域**
City Operations	城市运行
Government Relations	政府关系
Rights Protection	权益保护
Command, Control & Communications	指挥、控制、通信
Legal	法律
Operational Readiness	运行就绪
Planning & Coordination	计划与协调
Risk Management	风险管理

Signage (Wayfinding)	引导标识（指路标识）
Test Events Management	测试赛管理
Venue Management	场馆管理
Paralympic Games Integration	残奥整合
Accessibility	无障碍
Arrivals and Departures	抵离
Language Services	语言服务
NOC/NPC Services	国家 / 地区（残）奥委会服务
Olympic/Paralympic Family Services & Protocol	奥林匹克 / 残奥大家庭服务
Olympic/Paralympic Family Protocol	奥林匹克 / 残奥大家庭礼宾
Sport	体育
Sport Presentation	体育展示
Classification	分级
Brand, Identity & Look of The Games	品牌、形象和赛事景观
Broadcast Services	转播服务
Ceremonies	庆典仪式
City Activities & Live Sites	城市活动与文化广场
Communications	宣传
Culture	文化
Education	教育
Olympic/Paralympic Torch Relay	火炬传递
Press Operations	新闻运行
Cleaning and Waste	清洁与废弃物
Energy	电力
Legacy	遗产
Sustainability	可持续
Technology	技术
Venues and Infrastructure	场馆和基础设施
Business Development	商业开发
Finance	财务
Licensing	特许经营
Logistics	物流
Marketing Partner Services	市场合作伙伴服务
Procurement	采购
Ticketing	票务
Accommodation	住宿
Accreditation	注册
Doping Control	反兴奋剂

Information & Knowledge Management	信息和知识管理
Medical Services	医疗服务
People Management	人员管理
Security	安保
Spectator Experience	观众体验
Event Services	赛事服务
Transport	交通
Villages Management	奥运村管理
Volunteers	志愿者
Phases of Games	办赛阶段
Application Phase	申办阶段
Candidature Phase	候选阶段
Foundation Phase	基础规划阶段
Planning Phase	专项计划阶段
Readiness Phase	测试就绪阶段
Games Operation Phase	赛时运行阶段
Dissolution Phase	总结善后阶段
Plans	规划计划
Venues, Sports and Infrastructure Master Plan	场馆、体育和基础设施总体计划
Master Schedule	总体计划表
Milestone Tasks	里程碑任务
Marketing Plan	市场开发计划
Transition Communications Plan	过渡期宣传计划
Games Foundation Plan	赛事基础规划
Games Operation Plan	赛事运行规划
Strategic Risk Register	战略风险清单
Games Delivery Plan	赛事完成计划
Stakeholders Plan	利益相关方计划
Space Programmes & Design Briefs (Permanent)	空间规划及设计基本情况（永久）
Venue Concept Plans	场馆设计概念图
Model Venue Overlay Plan	示范场馆临建计划
Model Venue Operational Plan	示范场馆运行计划
Lifetime People Headcount	存续期人员编制
Contingency Plans	应急计划
City Integration Plan	城市整合计划
Operational Readiness Exercise Plan	运行就绪演练计划
C3 Co-Host Cities Plan	C3 协办城市计划
Licensing Pilot Plan	特许经营试运行计划

Olympic Movement	奥林匹克运动
Mount Olympus	奥林匹斯山
Olympia	奥林匹亚（希腊南部平原）
Olympic Museum	奥林匹克博物馆
Olympic Games, Olympics, Games of The Olympiad (Og)	奥林匹克运动会（奥运会）
Olympic Official Report	奥林匹克运动会官方报告
Olympic Mascot	奥林匹克运动会吉祥物
Olympic Games Global Impact (OGI/OGGI)	奥运会总体影响
Olympic Games Impact Study	奥运会总体影响研究
Goal of OGI Study	奥运会总体影响研究的目标
Evaluation of OGI Study	奥运会总体影响研究的衡量
OGI Indicators	奥运会总体影响研究的指标
Scope of OGI Study	奥运会总体影响研究的范围
Area of OGI Study	奥运会总体影响研究的规模
Time of OGI Study	奥运会总体影响研究的时间
Choice of OGI Research Partners	奥运会总体影响研究伙伴的选择
Objectivity of OGI Study	奥运会总体影响研究的客观性
Catalyst Effects of the Games	奥运会的促进效应
Olympic Legacy	奥运遗产
Transfer of Knowledge (TOK)	知识转移
Olympic Archives	奥运档案
Olympic City Legacy	奥运城市遗产
Olympic Motto	奥林匹克格言
Olympic Day	奥林匹克日
Pierre de Coubertin	皮埃尔·德·顾拜旦
Olympic Family Stand	奥林匹克大家庭座席
Olympic Knowledge Transfer	奥运会知识转让
Olympic Cultural Festival	奥林匹克文化节
Olympic Educational Activities	奥林匹克教育活动
Olympic Education Curriculum Resources	奥林匹克教育课程资源
Olympic Education Ticket Programme	奥林匹克教育票务计划
Olympic Education Wall Chart	奥林匹克教育知识挂图
Olympic Posters	奥林匹克宣传画
Olympic Reader	奥林匹克知识读本
Olympic Archives	奥运档案
Olympic Hospitality Centre	奥林匹克接待中心
Olympism	奥林匹克主义
Olympic Symbol	奥林匹克五环标志

Olympic Charter	奥林匹克宪章
Fundamental Principles of Olympism	奥林匹克主义的基本原则
Olympism Platform	奥林匹克主义纲领
Olympic Rings	奥林匹克五环
Olympic Flag	奥林匹克会旗
Olympic-Related Pictograms, Emblems,Signage and Designations	奥运会相关图标、会徽、标识和名称
International Olympic Committee (IOC)	国际奥委会
IOC Executive Board	国际奥委会执委会
IOC Games Management Team	国际奥委会奥运管理团队
IOC TOP Leadership Group (TLG)	国际奥委会全球合作伙伴领导小组
International Olympic Truce Centre (IOTC)	国际奥林匹克休战中心
IOC Headquarters	国际奥林匹克委员会总部
IOC Session	国际奥林匹克委员会全会
IOC Objective	国际奥林匹克委员会宗旨
IOC Composition	国际奥林匹克委员会的组成
IOC Official	国际奥林匹克委员会官员
IOC President	国际奥林匹克委员会主席
IOC Vice-President	国际奥林匹克委员会副主席
IOC Director General	国际奥林匹克委员会总干事
IOC Secretary General	国际奥林匹克委员会秘书长
IOC Olympic Games Executive Director	国际奥林匹克委员会奥运会部执行主任
IOC Honorary President	国际奥林匹克委员会名誉主席
IOC Honorary Member	国际奥林匹克委员会名誉委员
IOC Honour Member	国际奥林匹克委员会荣誉委员
IOC Technical Manual	国际奥林匹克委员会技术手册
IOC Official Languages	国际奥林匹克委员会官方语言
Eligibility of IOC Member	国际奥林匹克委员会委员的任职资格
Recruitment of IOC Members	国际奥林匹克委员会委员的物色
Election of IOC Members	国际奥林匹克委员会委员的选举
Admittance of IOC Members	国际奥林匹克委员会委员的确认
Status of IOC Members	国际奥林匹克委员会委员的地位
IOC Recognised Organisations	国际奥林匹克委员会承认的组织
Obligation of IOC Members	国际奥林匹克委员会委员的义务
IOC Honorary President for Life	国际奥林匹克委员会终身名誉主席
IOC Anti-Doping Rules	《国际奥林匹克委员会反兴奋剂规则》

IOC Olympic Prize for Sports Sciences	国际奥林匹克委员会奥林匹克体育科学奖
International Olympic Academy	国际奥林匹克学院
International Olympic Museum	国际奥林匹克博物馆
IOC Commissions	国际奥委会各专门委员会
IOC Sport and Law Commission	国际奥林匹克委员会体育与法律委员会
International Olympic Marketing Programme	国际奥林匹克市场开发计划
International Federation of Olympic Numismatic (FINO)	国际奥林匹克纪念币联合会
International Olympic Memorabilia Federation (FIMO)	国际奥林匹克纪念品联合会
IOC International Federation of Olympic Philately	国际奥林匹克委员会国际奥林匹克集邮联合会
IOC International Federation of Olympic Numismatics	国际奥林匹克委员会国际奥林匹克集币联合会
IOC Association of Collectors of Olympic Memorabilia	国际奥林匹克委员会奥林匹克纪念品收藏者协会
IOC Ethics Commission	国际奥林匹克委员会道德委员会
IOC Nominations Commission	国际奥林匹克委员会提名委员会
IOC Executive Board	国际奥林匹克委员会执行委员会
IOC Juridical Commission	国际奥林匹克委员会仲裁委员会
IOC Athletes' Commission	国际奥林匹克委员会运动员委员会
IOC Eligibility Commission	国际奥林匹克委员会资格审查委员会
IOC Women and Sport Commission	国际奥林匹克委员会妇女与体育委员会
IOC Working Group on Technology at the Olympic Games	国际奥林匹克委员会奥运会科技工作组
IOC Council of the Olympic Order	国际奥林匹克委员会奥林匹克勋章理事会
IOC Evaluation Commission	国际奥委会评估委员会
IOC Ethics Commission	国际奥委会道德委员会
IOC Olympic Collectors' Commission	国际奥林匹克委员会奥林匹克收藏者委员会
Olympic Philately, Numismatic and Memorabilia Commission	奥林匹克集邮、纪念币和纪念品委员会
Press Commission	新闻委员会
Olympic Programme Commission	奥林匹克项目委员会
Sport for All Commission	大众体育委员会
Olympic Solidarity Commission	团结基金委员会
The Commission for the International Olympic Academy	国际奥林匹克委员会国际奥林匹克学院委员会

Paralympics Movement	**残疾人奥林匹克运动**
Paralympic Movement	残疾人奥林匹克运动
Paralympic Games	残疾人奥林匹克运动会
Paralympic Motto	残疾人奥林匹克格言
Paralympic Symbol	残疾人奥林匹克标志
International Paralympic Committee	国际残疾人奥林匹克委员会
IPC General Assembly	国际残奥委会代表大会
IPC Member Organisation	国际残奥委会成员组织
IPC Governing Board	国际残奥委会理事会
International Paralympic Committee Headquarters	国际残奥委会总部
International Olympic Winter Sports Federation	**冬季奥运项目国际单项体育联合会**
International Biathlon Union (IBU)	国际冬季两项联盟
International Bobsleigh and Skeleton Federation (IBSF)	国际雪车联合会
World Curling Federation (WCF)	世界冰壶联合会
International Ice Hockey Federation (IIHF)	国际冰球联合会
International Skating Union (ISU)	国际滑冰联盟
International Luge Federation (FIL)	国际雪橇联合会
International Ski Federation (FIS)	国际滑雪联合会
NOC Associations	**国家和地区奥委会协会**
Association of National Olympic Committees （ANOC）	国家（地区）奥林匹克委员会总会
Association of National Olympic Committees of Africa (ACNOA)	非洲国家和地区奥林匹克委员会总会
Olympic Council of Asia (OCA)	亚奥理事会
The European Olympic Committees (EOC)	欧洲奥林匹克委员会
Pan-American Sports Organisation (PASO)	泛美体育组织
South American Sports Organisation	南美洲体育组织
Oceania National Olympic Committees (ONOC)	大洋洲奥林匹克委员会
Central American and Caribbean Sports Organisation (CACSO)	中美洲及加勒比海体育组织
Other Important International Sport Organisations	**其他重要国际体育组织**
Court of Arbitration for Sport (CAS)	体育仲裁法庭
World Anti-Doping Agency (WADA)	世界反兴奋剂机构
Media Operation	**媒体运行**
Olympic Channel Services	奥林匹克频道服务公司
Olympic Broadcast Services	奥林匹克转播服务公司
Rights-Holding Broadcaster	持权转播商
Press Rate Card	新闻收费卡
Press Conference Rooms	新闻发布厅
Press Work Room	文字记者工作间
Photographer Work Room	摄影记者工作间

Press Tribune	看台记者席
Photo Positions	摄影位置
Mixed Zone	混合区
Media Transport System	媒体交通系统
Bibs	（摄影、运动员）背心
Host Broadcaster	主转播商
Venue Production Director	场馆制片主任
Tracking Camera	转播摄像机（飞猫）
Beauty Camera	（城市）景观摄像机
Unilateral Feed	单边信号传输
Unilateral Broadcaster	单边转播机构
Multilateral Feed	多边信号传输
Multiple Television Screens	多屏电视墙
National Olympic Photo Pool (NOPP)	国家奥林匹克摄影队
Games Time Services	**赛时服务**
Accredited Seating	注册座席
Seating Bowl	座席区
Authorised Ticket Reseller	授权票务代理
T1/T2/T3 Transport Service	T1/T2/T3 交通服务
Pedestrian Screening Area	行人安检区
Vehicle Access and / or Parking Permit	车辆通行和 / 或停车证
Vehicle Screening Area	车辆安检区
Work as Directed Vehicles	按指令工作车辆
Transport Privileges and Priorities	交通特权及优先权
Precinct	周边地区
Passengers Wait，Embark or Disembark Their Vehicle	乘客候车、上车或下车
Sponsor Bump-In	赞助商入馆期
Sponsor Bump-Out	赞助商离馆期
Additional Team Officials	超编随队官员
Primary Team Officials	主要随队官员
Furniture, Fixtures and Equipment	家具、固定装置和设备
Prime Event Access	热点赛事通行权限
Pre-Valid Card	待激活身份注册卡
Load Zone	上下车站点
Chef de Mission Seminar	代表团团长会
Chef de Mission Dossier	代表团团长卷宗
Chef de Mission Meeting	代表团团长会议
Advance Team	先遣团队

Pre-Delegation Registration Meeting	代表团预注册会
High Demand Events	高需求赛事
Day Pass	一日卡
Daily Run Sheet	每日运行表
Sport Entries & Qualification	体育报名与资格审查
Olympic Family Vehicles	奥林匹克大家庭交通工具
Olympic Vehicle Route	奥林匹克车辆专用线路
Olympic Lane	奥林匹克车辆专用道
Olympic Transport Operations Centre (OTOC)	奥运会交通运行中心
Dedicated Olympic Shuttle Bus	奥运会专线客车
Dedicated Olympic Vehicle Traffic Lane	奥运会专用车道
Olympic Vehicle Access and/or Parking Permit (VAPP)	奥运会专用车证
Marketing	**市场开发**
Marketing Partner Coach Programme	市场开发合作伙伴培训计划
Marketing Partner Services	市场开发合作伙伴服务
Marketing Plan Agreement	市场开发计划协议
Joint Marketing Plan Agreement	联合市场开发计划协议
Marketing Revenues	市场开发收入
Marketing Agreement	市场开发协议
Marketing Communications	市场开发宣传
Concession	售卖点（特许）
Licensed Product	特许产品
Licensed Manufacturing and Retailing Right	特许经营权
Counterfeit Product	伪造品
Sponsorship in Cash	现金赞助
Communication and Market Values	宣传和市场价值
Sponsor Logo	赞助商标志
Sponsor Workshop	赞助商大会
Sponsor Guests	赞助商的客人
Sponsor Services	赞助商服务
Senior Executive of Sponsors	赞助商高级管理人员
Sponsor Accompanying Guest	赞助商陪同人员
Sponsor Recognition	赞助商识别
Chairman and CEO of Sponsor	赞助商主席和首席执行官
Ticketing	**票务**
Booking Office	订票处
Type II Tickets	二类门票
General Public Sales	公众销售

Ticket Exchange	换票
Ticket Rip Area (TRA)	检票区
Distribution of Tickets	门票分配
Purchasers of Games Tickets	门票购买者
Admission Ticket Programme	门票计划
Prices of The Tickets	门票价格
The Number of Available Tickets	门票数量
Price Zoning	票价分区制
General Sales Agent (GSA)	票务销售总代理
GSA Agreement	票务销售总代理协议
Thermal Tickets	热敏票
Ticket Soft Check (TSC)	软验票
Ticket Soft Check Point (TSC)	软验票点
Ticketing System	售票系统
Ticket Refund	退票
Ticket Check Point (TCP)	验票点
Type I Tickets	一类门票
On-Line Ticket Sales	在线售票
Main Ticketing Centre (MTC)	主票务中心
Victory Ceremony	**颁奖仪式**
Olympic Diploma	奥林匹克证书
Medal Presenter	颁奖嘉宾，颁奖人
Podium	颁奖台
Victory Ceremony Storage; Preparation Room for Podium	颁奖台存放室
Victory Ceremony (VC)	颁奖仪式
Victory Ceremony Waiting Area	颁奖仪式等候区
Victory Ceremony Manager Office & Storage Room for Medals	颁奖仪式经理办公室及奖牌存放间
Victory Ceremony Team (VCT)	颁奖仪式礼仪团队
Victory Ceremony Team Supervisor (VCTS)	颁奖仪式礼仪团队领队
Hair and Makeup Artist	化妆师
Medallist	获奖运动员
Presenter(s) Escort	嘉宾引导员
Flag-Bearer	升旗手 / 护旗手
Medal/Flower Bearer	托盘礼仪人员
Flower	鲜花
Silver Medal	银牌
Athletes Escort	运动员引导员
Diploma	证书

Torch Relay	火炬传递
Quiver	火炬背包
Shape of the Torch	火炬式样
Torch Gas Canister	火炬燃料罐
Torch Adaptor	火炬适配器
Lighting Ceremony	火炬点火仪式
Olympic Torch Relay Centre (OTRC)	火炬接力中心
Imagery of the Torch Relay	火炬传递形象
Torch Relay Route	火炬传递路线
Announcement of the Route of the Torch Relay	火炬传递路线发布
Torch Relay Task Force	火炬传递工作组
Torch Relay Providers	火炬传递供应商
Look of the Relay	火炬传递景观
Elements of the Relay	火炬传递景观标准
Relay Presenting Partners	火炬传递具名合作伙伴
Olympic Torch Relay Sponsorship Participants	火炬接力赞助计划参与者
Torchbearer Identification Number	火炬手编号
Torchbearer Pick Up Shuttle	火炬手收集车
Torchbearer Collection Point	火炬手收集点
Torchbearer Database	火炬手数据库
Torchbearer Drop Off Shuttle	火炬手投放车
The Selection Criteria for the Olympic Torchbearers	火炬手选拔标准
Torchbearer Envelope	火炬手传递区域
Torchbearer Leg	火炬手接力路段
Torchbearer Segment	火炬手接力路段分段
Torchbearer Slotting	火炬手传递路段分配
Safety Lantern	火种灯
Safety Lantern Fuel	火种灯燃料
Lantern Cradle	火种灯托盘
Lantern Carry Box	火种灯携带箱
Logistics & Procurement	**物流和采购**
Procurement	采购
Purchase Order	采购订单
Purchase Methods	采购方式
Procurement Agent	采购中介代理机构
Transfer Request (TR)	调拨申请
Delivery List (DL)	调度清单
Decentralized procurement	分散采购

Allocation Criteria	分配标准
Allocation Procedure	分配程序
Distribution System	分配系统
Distribution Centre (DC)	分配中心
Suppliers	供应商
Logistic Service Centre	物流服务中心
Reverse Logistics Service	逆向物流服务
Logistics	物流
Materials Transfer Area (MTA)	物流区
Logistics Centre	物流中心
Logistics Manager	物流经理
Bump-out	物资移出
Stock Keep Unit (SKU)	库存单品
Inventory Controller (IC)	库存管理员
Movement Request (MR)	库存移动请求
Warehouse Management System (WMS)	仓库管理系统
Accreditation	注册
Olympic Identity and Accreditation Card (OIAC)	奥林匹克身份注册卡
Venue Accreditation Office	场馆注册办公室
Code	代码
Pre-Valid Card (PVC)	待激活身份注册卡
Guest Pass	访客卡
Zone Code	分区代码
Closed Venue	封闭式场馆
Validation	激活
Transferable Accreditation	可转让的注册证件
Quota	配额
Access Rights	（通行）权限
Prime Event Access (PEA)	热点赛事通行
Upgrade Card	升级卡
Properly Accredited	顺利注册
Upgrade Pass	提升证件级别
Bar Code	条形码
Access Control	通行控制
Photo Library	图片库
Work Schedule	班次安排
Application Period	报名时间
Privilege	优待权

Validation	有效期
Main Accreditation Centre (MAC)	主注册中心
Accredited Seating Area	注册座席区
The Number of Accredited Seats	注册座席数量
Accreditation Category	注册类别
Transport	交通
Ticket Check	检票
Entry Control	进入控制
Barricade	路障
Shift	轮班
Daily Run Sheet	每日运行表
Night Flight	夜间航班
Staging Area	暂停区
Depot Management	站点管理
Branch Road	支路
Direct and Dedicated Transport Service	直达以及专用交通服务
Way-Finding Signage	指路标识
Centre Zone	中心区
Mini-Bus	小型客车
Trunk Road	主干路
Professional Driver	专业司机
(Dedicated) Vehicle	专用车辆
(Dedicated) Driver	专职司机
Transport Hub	交通枢纽
Games Transport Operations and Services	赛时交通运行服务
Metro and Tramway	地铁和有轨电车
Shuttle Bus	班车
Olympic Lane	奥运专用车道
Travel Times	行车时间
Transport System	交通系统
Transport Links	交通联络线
“Games Train”	奥运专列
Transport Logistics Hub	交通物流枢纽
Transport Scheme	交通计划
Olympic Vehicle Access & Parking Permit (VAPP)	奥运会专用车证
Olympic Constituent Group Allocated Vehicles	奥运会组成团队的车辆配备
Olympic Transport Services Level	奥运交通服务等级

Olympic Traffic Information and Communication Service System	奥运交通信息服务系统
Olympic Traffic Contingency Control Centre	奥运交通应急指挥中心
Olympic Transport Impact	奥运交通影响
Olympic Transport Operation Centre (OTOC)	奥运交通运行中心
Olympic Transport Route	奥运线路
Olympic Dedicated and Direct Shuttle (DDS)	奥运专项直达专线客车
Olympic Dedicated Passageway	奥运专用通道
Olympic Bus Line	奥运公交专线
Accommodation	住宿
Accommodation System	住宿系统
Accommodation Allocation Agreement (AAA)	住宿分配协议
Tourist Nights	游客宿夜天数
Star Category	星级
Massage Room	按摩室
Lobby	大堂
Hotel Category	饭店级别
Service Level Agreement (SLA)	服务水平协议
Doping Control	反兴奋剂
Olympic Anti-doping Laboratory (OAL)	奥运会兴奋剂检测中心
Olympic Doping Control Operation Centre	奥运会兴奋剂控制运行中心
Specific Gravity	比重
Stimulants	刺激类
Marijuana	大麻
Anabolic Agents	蛋白同化制剂
Processing Room	分析室
Waiting Room	候检室
Health Blood Control	健康血检
Prohibited Substance and Method	禁用物质与方法
Breath Alcohol Test	酒精呼吸检测
Local Anesthetics	局部麻醉剂
Disposable Material	可分解物质
Diuretics	利尿剂
Narcotics	麻醉剂
Urine Sample	尿样
Corticosteroids	皮质类固醇
In-Competition Testing	赛内检查
Pre-Competition Testing	赛前检查

WADA Independent Observer	世界反兴奋剂机构独立观察员
Doping Control Officer	兴奋剂检查官
Doping Control Registrar	兴奋剂检查进出控制员
Medical Services	医疗服务
Medical Services at the Olympic Hospitals	定点医院医疗服务
Dull Ache	钝痛，闷痛
Polyclinic	多功能诊所
Fever	发烧，发热
Inflammation	发炎
Reflexes	反应，反射动作
Relax (Muscle)	放松（肌肉）
Side Effects	副作用
Cold	感冒
Joint	关节
Arthritis	关节炎
Disposable Material	耗材
Sore Throat	喉咙痛
Respiratory Disorders	呼吸系统疾病
Hay Fever Preparations	花粉热制剂
Recurrent	回归动脉（神经）
Tendonitis	肌腱炎
Muscle Strain	肌肉劳损
Muscle Contract	肌肉收缩
Laser Therapy	激光治疗
First Aid Kit	急救包
Emergency Medical Service (EMS)	急救服务系统
Emergent Physician	急救医生
Acute	急性的
Spine	脊柱
Spina Bifida	脊柱裂
Dosage	剂量
Splint	夹板
Anxiety	焦虑
Throbbing Pain	绞痛与搏动性痛
Contraindications	禁忌症候
Ambulance Officer	救护主任
General Anesthesia	全身麻醉
Severe Pain	剧痛

Anti-Infective Drugs	抗感染药物
Cough	咳嗽
Physiotherapist	理疗师
Strength	力量
Compression	压迫，受压；压迫法
Medication	药疗法，投药法
Medical Evacuation	医疗护送
Emergency Services System	医疗急救网络
Medical Facility	医疗设施
Medical Staff	医疗卫生人员
Medical Supplies	医疗用品
Medical Care	医药卫生
Bruise	瘀伤
Medical Station For Athletes	运动员医疗站
Adhesions	粘连
Sedatives	镇静剂
Spinal Manipulation	整脊术
Anti-Diarrheal	止泻药
Medicinal Herbs	中草药
Swelling	肿胀
Podiatry	足病学
Security	**安保**
Olympic Security Command Centre; Security Command Centre (SCC)	安保指挥中心
Security Assistant	安保助理
Mag & Bag	安检
Olympic Games Security Plan	奥运会安全计划
Enclosed Zone	安保封闭区
Secure Perimeter	安保封闭线
Security Service Vehicle	安保服务车
Security Expenses	安保服务费用
Security Overlay	安保覆盖区域
Security Motorcyclist	安保摩托车手
Security Personnel	安保人员
Security Operations	安保运行
Security Volunteer	安保志愿人员
Screening Point Design	安检口设计
Level of Security	安全保障级别

Security Screening	安全检查
Security Assembly Area	安全聚集场所
Security Control Centre	安全控制中心
Fire Brigade Garage	消防车库
Fire Brigade	消防队
Fire Station	消防站
Zone Control Point (ZCP)	区域控制点
International Criminal Police Organisation/ Interpol (ICPO)	国际刑警组织
Air Traffic Control System	空中管制系统
Olympic Village	奥运村
Village Allotment Process	村内分配程序
Village Services	村内服务
Bus Routes in the Olympic Village	村内公共汽车路线
PRD Supervisor (PRD SPV)	打印分发主管
Storage Area and Workshops for Delegates	代表团的贮藏间、维修间
Public Open-air Leisure Areas	公共户外休闲地
Entrance to the International Zone	国际区入口
Laundry Facility	洗衣设施
Athlete Apartments	运动员公寓
Food & Beverage	食品与饮料
Food Processing Centre	食品加工中心
Kiosk; Newsstand	书报亭
Private Rental Space	租用工作间
Pre-Delegation Registration Meeting (Pre-DRM)	先遣代表团登记会议
Client Registration Process (CRP)	客户登记流程
Village Planning and Operation Department	奥运村部
Pre-planned Services	预订服务
Residential Zone (RZ)	居住区
NOC Service Centre	NOC 服务中心
Olympic Village Polyclinic	奥运村综合诊所
Super Resident Centre	超级居民中心
Chef de Mission Office	代表团团长办公室
Chefs de Mission Meeting	代表团团长例会
Delegation Registration Meeting	代表团注册会议
Village Opening	开村
Village Closing	闭村
Gymnasium / Fitness Centre	健身房
Sports Complex	健身区

Housekeeping	客房服务
Jogging Route	慢跑道
Sports Information Centre	体育信息中心
Team Office	团队办公室
Lounge Area	休息区
Olympic Village Plaza (OVP)	国际区
Mayor' s Room	村长办公室
Mayor' s Office	村长院
Calling Centre	电信服务中心
Dry Cleaning	干洗店
Welcome Ceremony Stage	欢迎仪式舞台
Courier Service	快递服务
Protocol Tour	礼宾参观
Tourism Information Centre	旅游信息中心
Flag Mall	升旗广场
Cultural Showcase	文化展示
Information Station	信息服务站
General Store	综合商店
Operational Zone (OZ)	运行区
Olympic Village Guide	《奥运村指南》
NOC Dedicated Vehicle	专用车辆
Lock-Down	安保锁闭
Olympic Village Signage Policy (OVSP)	奥运村标识政策
Village Management Office (VMO)	奥运村管理办公室
Internal Shuttle Bus	奥运村内班车
Village Layout	奥运村平面图
Olympic Village Communication Centre	奥运村通信中心
Olympic Village Operation Centre	奥运村运行中心
Paralympic Winter Games	**冬残奥会**
Classification	分级
Classification Form	分级表
Classification Panel	分级工作组
Classification Process	分级过程
Classification Protest	分级抗议
Classification Protest Panel	分级抗议工作组
Classification Master List	分级列表
Classification Evaluation Period	分级评定阶段
Classification Assessment	分级评估

Classification Evaluation Period	分级评估期间
Classification Appeal	分级申诉
Classifier	分级师
Classification Room	分级室
Classification System	分级系统
Classification Coordination Centre (CCC)	分级协调中心
Classification Master List	分级信息汇总表
Classification Requirement	分级需求
Classification Panel	分级专家组
Classification Status	分级状态
Acquired Amputation	后天截肢（获得性截肢）
Spinal Cord Injury Class	脊髓损伤级别
Spinal Cord Injury	脊髓损伤
Orthotics and Prosthetics	矫形器和假肢
Shoulder Elbow Wrist Hand Orthosis (SEWHO)	肩肘腕手矫形器
Orthotic and Prosthetic Repair	矫形器和假肢修理
Prosthetic Foot	假足
Foot Propelled Wheelchair	脚踏轮椅
Prosthesis Athlete	戴假肢的运动员
Paraplegia	截瘫
Amputee	被截肢者
Amputee Class	截肢级别
Wheelchair and Prosthetic Repair Centre	轮椅和假肢维修中心
Wheelchair Repair	轮椅维修
Wheelchair Repair Service	轮椅维修服务
Wheelchair Athlete	轮椅运动员
Tactile Surface Indication Roadway	盲道
White Cane	盲杖
Ramp	坡道
Limbs	上下肢
Upper Limbs	上肢
Upper Limb Amputation	上肢截肢
Upper Limb Amputee Athlete	上肢截肢运动员
Visual Impairment	视觉障碍
Visually Impaired	视力残疾
Visual Impairment Class	视力障碍级别
Diminished Visual Field	视野缩小
Arm Prosthesis	上肢假肢

Bilateral Amputee Athlete	双侧截肢运动员
Diplegia	双肢瘫痪
Quadriplegia	四肢麻痹
Tetraplegia; Quadriplegia	四肢瘫
Accessible Bus	无障碍大巴
Accessible Environment	无障碍环境
Beneficiary of an Accessible Environment	无障碍环境的受益者
Accessibility and Disability Awareness	无障碍及残疾意识
Accessible Platform	无障碍平台
The Right to Access	无障碍权利
Accessible Equipment	无障碍设备
Accessible Facilities	无障碍设施
Accessible Pavement; Accessible Path	无障碍通道
Accessible Seat	无障碍座席
Above-Knee Amputation	膝以上截肢
Below-Knee Amputation	膝以下截肢
Lower Limb Amputation	下肢截肢
Unilateral Ankle Amputation	一侧踝关节截肢
Re-Classify	重新分级
Above-Elbow Amputation	肘以上截肢
Below-Elbow Amputation	肘以下截肢
Chief Classifier	主分级师
Competition	竞赛
Sport Services	竞赛服务
Competition Management	竞赛管理
Competition Cancellation	竞赛取消
Competition Delay	竞赛推迟
Sport Training	竞赛训练
Competition Postponement	竞赛延期
Sport Operations	竞赛运行
Sport Manager	竞赛主任
Competition Schedule	竞赛日程表
Sport Entry Form	竞赛报名表
Sport Publications	体育出版物
Timekeeping	计时
Scoreboard	记分牌
Room for the Scoring	记分室
Technical Official (TO)	技术官员

National Technical Official	国内技术官员
International Technical Officials (ITOs)	国际技术官员
Competition Office	竞赛办公室
Sport Volunteers	竞赛志愿者
Sport Command Centre (SCC)	竞赛指挥中心
Competition Support Area	竞赛保障区域
Field of Play Specification	竞赛场馆细则
Sport Entries Deadline	竞赛报名终止日期
Sports Entries & Qualification (SEQ)	竞赛报名与资格审查
Main Design Standards for Accessibility in A Competition Venue	竞赛场馆无障碍的主要标准
Sport Entries & Qualification Manual (SEQ Manual)	竞赛报名与资格审查手册
Rules of Timing	计时规则
Timing & Scoring Systems (T&S)	计时和计分系统
Timing, Scoring and Result Service	计时、计分和成绩服务
Call Area	检录区
Official Weigh-in Room	称重间
Venue Management	场馆管理
Venuisation	场馆化
Venue Cluster	场馆群
Off-Venue Areas	场馆外区域
Venue Matrices	场馆分区表
Venue Look	场馆景观
Venue Development	场馆开发
Venue Construction	场馆建设
Venue Adaptation	场馆改建
Front of House (FOH)	场馆前院
Back of House (BOH)	场馆后院
Venue Team	场馆团队
Venue Operation	场馆运行
Venue Operation Procedure	场馆运行程序
Venue Operational Design	场馆运行设计
Venue Operation Manual	场馆运行手册
Venue Operation Policy	场馆运行政策
Venue Operation Centre (VOC)	场馆运行中心
Venue Functional Operations	场馆职能运行
Secretary General of Venue Operations	场馆运行秘书长
Venue Integrated Schedule	场馆运行进度计划

Venue Preliminary Operational Design	场馆初步运行设计
Venue Detailed Operational Design	场馆详细运行设计
Daily Run Sheet (DRS)	场馆每日运行时间表
Venue and Infrastructure Construction Schedule (VICS)	场馆及基础设施建设进度表
Venue Contingency Plan	场馆应急预案
Exclusive Access Period	场馆独家使用期
Audio Venue Technician	场馆音频设备技术员
Vice Venue Manager	场馆副主任
Venue Broadcasting Manager (VBM)	场馆广播经理
Venue Protocol Manager	场馆礼宾经理
Vice Venue Manager (Support)	场馆后勤副主任
Vice Venue Protocol Manager	场馆礼宾副经理
Assistant of Venue Technical Manager	场馆技术经理助理
Vice Venue Manager (Media)	场馆媒体副主任
Venue Media Centres (VMCs)	场馆媒体中心
Venue Media Centres Operating Plan	场馆媒体中心运行计划
Venue Master Plan	场馆总体计划
Venue Planning Principles	场馆规划原则
Venue Gross Capacity	场馆总座
Venue Human Resources	场馆人事
Venue Staffing Plan	场馆人员计划
Venues & Facilities	场馆和设施
Site Management Manager	场馆设施管理经理
Venue Photo Service	场馆摄影服务
On-Site Simulation	场馆实地演练
Venue Specific Training	场馆专项训练
Venue Communications	场馆通信
Venue Communications Centre (VCC)	场馆通信中心
Venue Access Codes	场馆通行代码
Venue Stuff Plan	场馆物资计划
Venue Local Support	场馆外围保障
Venue Soft Domain	场馆外围保障区域
Venue Local Support Team	场馆外围保障工作组
Vice Venue Manager (Local Relations)	场馆属地关系副主任
Legal Affairs	**法律事务**
WADA Copenhagen Declaration	世界反兴奋剂机构哥本哈根宣言
UNESCO International Convention	联合国教科文组织国际公约
Olympic Law	奥林匹克法
Host City Contract	主办城市合同

International Plant Protection Convention (IPPC)	国际植物保护公约
International Trademark Rights	国际商标权
IOC Legal Status	国际奥林匹克委员会的法律地位
WADA Copenhagen Declaration	世界反兴奋剂机构哥本哈根宣言
Regulations on Protection of Olympic Symbols	奥林匹克标志保护条例
Exclusive Right	独家权利
Legal Protection	法律保护
Legal Guarantee	法律保障
Legal Framework	法律框架
Legal Entity	法律实体
Status of A Legal Person	法人地位
Olympic Education	**奥林匹克教育**
Olympic Educational Activities	奥林匹克教育活动
Olympic Education Ticket Programme	奥林匹克教育票务计划
Olympic Education Curriculum Resources	奥林匹克教育课程资源
Olympic Education Wall Chart	奥林匹克教育知识挂图
Olympic Youth Camp	奥林匹克青年营
Olympic Photographic Archive Bureau (OPAB)	奥林匹克图片档案署
Olympic Books	奥林匹克图书
Olympic Summer Camp	奥林匹克夏令营
Opening & Closing Ceremonies	**开闭幕式**
Head of State Entry	国家元首入场
Playing the National Anthem	奏国歌
Fanfare	进行曲（开幕式、闭幕式）
Amenity	礼仪
Parade of Athletes	运动员入场
Dove Release	放飞和平鸽
OCOG President' s Speech	组委会主席致辞
IOC President' s Speech	国际奥委会主席致辞
Raising the Olympic Flag and Playing the Olympic Anthem	升奥林匹克会旗、奏奥林匹克会歌
Athletes' Oath	运动员宣誓
Officials' Oath	裁判员宣誓
Lighting of the Olympic Flame	点燃奥林匹克圣火
Protocol Order of the Closing Ceremony	闭幕式程序
Entry of Nations' (Territories') Flags	国旗（会旗）入场
Flag Handover Ceremony	奥林匹克会旗交接仪式
Next Host City Artistic Segment	下届举办城市艺术表演
Exit of the Olympic Flag	奥林匹克会旗退场
Extinguishing of the Olympic Flame	熄灭奥林匹克圣火